In Spirit And In Truth

The Call of True Worship

Copyright © – Courtney Laird – 2025

All rights reserved

ISBN: 978-0-6488463-6-9

All rights reserved. No part of this publication may be reproduced, stored in a retrieval system, or transmitted in any form or by any means mechanical, electronic, photocopying or otherwise without the express written permission of the author.

The author can be contacted at:

courtney.a.laird@gmail.com

Scripture references are taken from:

The Authorised King James version of the Bible

The New King James version of the Bible © 1982 Thomas Nelson. Inc. Used by permission. All rights reserved.

Words of scripture written in bold are used by the writer for specific emphasis.

Dedication

To my three amazing children; Isaiah, Grace and Petyon. Words cannot express the incredible blessings that you are and the joy that you bring to my life daily. Being your dad is an absolute privilege and one that I am incredibly grateful for. It has been a blessing to watch you grow over the years and I am so excited for what lays ahead in each of your lives. My life is truly richer because of you three.

Much love,

Dad

Contents

Introduction	1
A Call to True Worship	5
The Standard of True	33
In Flesh Or In Spirit	51
Worship in Flesh	55
Worship in Spirit	77
Identifying the Flesh in our Worship.	101
Reflection	121
In Error Or In Truth	127
Worship in Error	145
Worship in Truth	157
Identifying Error in our Worship	169
Reflection	187
It Takes Both!	193
The Lord is Seeking	211
Final Thoughts	213
Bibliography	219

Introduction

This study was birthed over a period of several months, as I felt the Lord impress upon my heart the words of Jesus in John 4:24:

> *"God is Spirit, and those who worship Him must worship in Spirit and Truth."*

Initially this was just a seed, a verse that was ruminating in my spirit and one that couldn't be shaken. Then one Sunday morning as I listened to a sermon, the Lord began to cause the seed to sprout and grow. The sermon itself was unrelated to this topic, but as I sat and listened with a teachable spirit to what was being communicated, the Lord germinated the seed within me and caused it to grow. A teachable spirit can be defined as having ears to hear what the Lord would say, without any bias towards the message or the messenger. It is a focus not just on what the person is saying, but also on what is the Lord speaking to me through this. It is a position of humility with a desire to learn and grow in truth. When we have an open teachable spirit to the things of God, we make room for His Spirit to minister to us.

In the proceeding hours of that Sunday, the outline of this text very quickly came together as the Lord supplied the puzzle pieces and started to align them. The message of this text is one that the I strongly feel is for both believers and the Church of today. I believe that we are in a season of refining and preparation and that the Lord is wanting His Church to ready herself for what is to come. In this time the Church is being stirred

INTRODUCTION

by the Father to check her course, correct if necessary and make sure that she is fully aligned with the foundational truths of the faith.

My prayer is that you would be both blessed and challenged as you read through this study. You may not agree with everything that is written, and my own inadequacies may not properly communicate that which the Lord has put on my heart. But if you can maintain a teachable spirit as you read it, you will allow the Holy Spirit to fully minister His truth regardless of what has been written.

Before we start, would you pray with me:

> *Lord, as I began to read through this text would you help me to have a teachable spirit. Would you please soften my heart and remove any personal walls or biases that I have established.*
>
> *Holy Spirit, I ask that you speak to me as I read and quicken to me any truth that I need to hear. Would you please help me to hear **Your** message through text. Help me look beyond the human inadequacies of the message and the messenger and have a heart to receive **Your** truth.*
>
> *Lord, I pray, that you would help me to be one who worships in spirit and in truth.*
>
> *In Jesus name,*
>
> *Amen.*

Blessings in Christ,

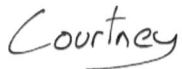

A Look at Worship

A Call to True Worship

In John chapter 4 we read that Jesus had left Judea and was heading towards Galilee. His journey took Him through the region of Samaria, in particular to the city of Sychar where Jacob's well was located. Being wearied from His journey, Jesus sat down by Jacob's well to rest while the disciples went into town to buy provisions. As Jesus sat and waited, He was met by a Samaritan woman who had come to draw water from the well. This encounter is beautifully portrayed in the series, 'The Chosen', and is a scene that has played through my mind continually as I composed this text.

Our focus in this text is not so much on the encounter itself, but rather on the conversation that transpired between Jesus and the Samaritan woman in vs 19 to 26. Whilst within this passage we read of Jesus revealing Himself as the Messiah to the Samaritan woman, we also pick up our topic of focus. Within these seven verses the term worship is mentioned some ten times, as highlighted below:

> The woman said to Him, "Sir, I perceive that You are a prophet. Our fathers **worshiped** on this mountain, and you Jews say that in Jerusalem is the place where one ought to **worship**." Jesus said to her, "Woman, believe Me, the hour is coming when you will neither on this mountain, nor in Jerusalem, **worship** the Father. You **worship** what you do not know; we know what we **worship**, for salvation is of the Jews. But the hour is

> *coming, and now is, when the true **worshipers** will **worship** the Father in spirit and truth; for the Father is seeking such to **worship** Him. God is Spirit, and those who **worship** Him must **worship** in spirit and truth." The woman said to Him, "I know that Messiah is coming" (who is called Christ). "When He comes, He will tell us all things." Jesus said to her, "I who speak to you am He." (Joh 4:19-26) NKJV*

There can be no missing the clear focus within this passage. Worship is at the heart of these verses. It is mentioned and re-mentioned numerous times, with Jesus directly mentioning worship some eight times in just four verses. There is an emphasis on worship here that the Lord is wanting His people to see, and grasp hold of.

In order to understand what is being said in this passage, we will start by examining the conversation that transpired between the Samaritan woman and Jesus before then more fully looking at the term worship as it is used in this passage. As we do this, we will start to build an understanding of the true worship that Jesus was speaking of.

The Conversation

Immediately after the Samaritan woman recognised Jesus to be a prophet, she brought up the topic of worship:

> *The woman said to Him, "Sir, I perceive that You are a prophet. Our fathers **worshiped** on this mountain, and you Jews say that in Jerusalem is the place where one ought to **worship**." (Joh 4:19-20) NKJV*

In essence what the Samaritan woman was saying was "our fathers worshipped at such and such a place but you Jews say we ought to worship at another". To put it another way, "we worship like this, but you say that it's wrong". We are reading here of an issue of division that had separated the worship of the Samaritans from that of the worship of the Jews. It was something that had caused conflict, contention and disagreement between the two nations.

It is interesting that when we read the encounter between the Samaritan woman and Jesus in its entirety, this statement of the Samaritan woman regarding worship seems so out of place within the context of the passage. The two had been conversing back and forth about water. Jesus had just told the Samaritan woman how she had had five husbands and that the man she was now with was not her husband. The Samaritan woman had perceived Jesus to be a prophet, and it was only after having this revelation that she then launched into this statement about worship. As I pondered this, the thought that kept coming into my mind was why this segway? Why this sudden shift to worship? Why was it only when she perceived Jesus to be a man of God that the conversation then took this turn? From the very start she knew Jesus to be a Jew, but that had never prompted her to bring worship up in the conversation. So why did she now?

For me this speaks to the heart of the Samaritan woman. She had just identified Jesus to be a prophet of the Lord, which in itself was a marvellous thing. Israel had been in the four hundred silent years period since Malachi, where there were no recognised prophetic voices. This woman though perceived Jesus to be a prophet and interestingly the very next thing that she did was to pose this question. The division that existed over worship was something that troubled her. It was something that she didn't fully understand or comprehend but she had a **HEART** to know more.

In response to this question of the Samaritan woman, Jesus did three things:

JESUS ADDRESSED THE ISSUE OF DIVISION.

Jesus said to her, "Woman, believe Me, the hour is coming when you will **neither on this mountain, nor in Jerusalem, worship the Father.** *(vs21) NKJV*

But the hour is coming, and now is... (vs23)

Jesus was saying that the hour would soon come when the place of worship would not be the focus of worship. The Samaritan woman's issue had centred around the place of worship, where it occurred. The Samaritans worshipped on this mount, but the Jews said worship must be done in Jerusalem. The division centred around the place where worship was to occur. It was a point of contention. Jesus, in one sentence, stated that the issue which was causing the division, soon wouldn't be an issue. It wouldn't be about Jerusalem, and it wouldn't be about any mountain. In fact, it was not going to be about a place at all.

Notice though the emphasis that Jesus added. The Samaritan woman hadn't mentioned worship of the Father, she just had mentioned worship. Jesus though emphasised who should be worshipped. We will explore this more fully in our next point.

JESUS GOT TO THE ROOT OF THE ISSUE.

> *You **worship** what you do not know; we know what we **worship**, for salvation is of the Jews (vs 22). NKJV*

The words of Jesus here may seem a little harsh, and in order to for us to understand what He was saying and why He was saying it, we need to look at the history of Samaria. Samaria was once a town of Israel. During the reign of king Rehoboam, Solomon's son, the nation of Israel was divided into two kingdoms, the kingdom of Israel and the kingdom of Judah. The house of David maintained their rulership over the kingdom of Judah, but the kingdom of Israel became subject to king Jeroboam. When Jeroboam took the throne of Israel, he was afraid that if the people kept going to worship in Jerusalem, which was in the kingdom of Judah, their allegiance may turn back to the house of David. To avoid this happening, king Jeroboam set up two golden calves for the people to go and worship before, one in Bethel and the other in Dan. The people immediately adopted the king's practices and adhered to the false feasts that he also introduced. It was the start of the people of Israel moving away from the Lord.

Years later because of the sins of the kings of Israel and the sins of the people themselves, the nation was taken captive by the king of Assyria. Whilst the kingdom of Judah suffered a similar fate under Babylon, after 70 years captivity they would return to the land. The people of the kingdom of Israel though never again returned to their homeland. Samaria was resettled by the king of Assyria with people from other nations. This is detailed for us in 2 Kings 17:24-41 and I would encourage you to read over this passage before moving forward.

In 2 Kings 17 we read that the people who were settled in the land did not fear the Lord and so the Lord sent lions amongst the people as judgement. In response to this judgement of the Lord, the people pleaded with the king of Assyria as they did not know how to appease the gods of the land. They did not know the correct rituals and so were being punished. In response to this the king of Assyria sent them one of the priests of Israel, to dwell in Bethel and to teach the people how to fear the Lord. The result of this was that the people learned how to fear the Lord, but they never actually forsook their own gods. Each nation of people worshipped the Lord, but they also worshipped their own gods as well:

> ***They feared the Lord, yet served their own gods –***
> *according to the rituals of the nations from among whom they were carried away (vs 33). NKJV*

They feared the Lord, yet they served their own gods. They had a foot in both camps and were trying to serve two masters. Samaria was a place of mixture. They weren't committed to the Lord, they just sought to appease Him whilst not changing anything else. The Lord was just another one of the gods that they worshipped. This is why Jesus references the worship of the Father is verses 21 and 23 and it is also why He stated that the Samaritans did not know what they worshipped whereas the Jews did. The Jews may have been bound up in the law, but they knew who God was and they knew that He alone was God. There was not mixture with them as there was with the Samaritans.

The issue lay not with the place of worship, but rather with the knowing of who they worshipped.

JESUS ADDRESSED WHAT WORSHIP IS.

Having addressed the issue of the place of worship, Jesus then expounded to the woman what worship is:

> *But the hour is coming, and now is, when* ***the true worshipers will worship the Father in spirit and truth****; for the Father is seeking such to worship Him. God is Spirit, and* ***those who worship Him must worship in spirit and truth.****" (Joh 4:23-24) NKJV*

Jesus had taken care of the issue of division of where worship was to occur. He had then realigned the woman with who she was to worship, i.e. the Father. Jesus then told her how this worship was to be done. Worship was not to be a religious ceremony but rather something that was to be done by individuals in spirit and in truth. In the verses above we can see that Jesus repeated this message. Twice He said that true worship was to be done in spirit and truth. There are no wasted words in scripture. The Word is divinely written, and when something like this is repeated it is because it is meant **to get our attention**. There is an emphasis here that the Lord is wanting us to pick up on. This is something that we will explore more fully in the coming chapters. For now, what we need to grab hold of is that Jesus defined true worship as worship that is done in spirit and in truth. This is what the Father is looking for!

It is interesting to note that such was the power in Jesus' response to the woman's question, that she jumped from Him being a prophet of the Lord to raising the question of Messiahship. So powerful was the message she received that something changed within her. In this very short space of time Jesus had gone from being a man, to a Jew, to being a prophet to now possibly being the Messiah! Notice that when Jesus revealed Himself, the woman never questioned! There was no doubt in her mind. Jesus literally fulfilled His own words of John 4:14.

> *but whoever drinks of the water that I shall give him will never thirst. But the water that I shall give him will become in him a fountain of water springing up into everlasting life." (Joh 4:14) NKJV*

The woman was parched in the area of worship but went away having received the living water and had a fountain spring up in her as she went and spread the news to her village. This was an amazing encounter and one that revolved around the theme of worship!

Within this passage of John 4:19-26 we discover a revelation of true worship. Jesus sought to take away the division of worship that was a strong hold in the mind of the Samaritan woman and impart to her a greater understanding of what true worship is.

As a point of interest, notice that Jesus set aside both the worship of the Samaritans and the worship of the Jews.

> *Jesus said to her, "Woman, believe Me, the hour is coming* **when you will neither on this mountain, nor in Jerusalem,** *worship the Father. (Joh 4:21) NKJV*

Having set aside the former, Jesus then laid out truth. True worship consists of true worshippers worshipping the Father in spirit and in truth. True worship is worship that is in spirit and in truth.

The Term

Having seen how the encounter from John 4 focused in on the theme of worship, we now turn our attention to understanding what is meant by the term worship in the above context. We have already noted that the word worship is used some ten times between verses 20 and 24. What is interesting to note is that in nine of these instances the same Greek word, "proskyneo", is used. The definition for this word according to Strongs Exhaustive Concordance is quoted here in full and I would encourage you to read over this several times and pause to consider this definition in light of what Jesus was saying.

> *Proskyneo: From G4314 and probably a derivative of G2965 (meaning to kiss, like a dog licking his master's hand); to fawn or crouch to, i.e. (literally or figuratively) prostrate oneself in homage (do reverence to, adore): - worship.*

When I first read and contemplated this, I was a little taken back. As believers we generally have some preconceived thoughts on worship, but the definitions reference to "like a dog licking his master's hand" is possibly not something that we would immediately associate with worship. In some ways it is a jarring definition. The more that I thought about this though, the more I was prompted that this was the word that Jesus deliberately and purposefully chose to use repeatedly in defining what worship is. This is not something that can be simply explained away, this was the message that Jesus wanted His people to get hold of. He wanted us to grasp the truth of this so much that He repeated the same word over and over. There were other words that Jesus could have used but He didn't! Jesus defined this as the type of worship that the Father is seeking and the worship that true worshippers offer. As a dog licks its master hand, so do true worshippers worship the Father. This definition reveals to us that worship is not just an action, it is also a position and an attitude literally, physically and spiritually.

The Example

As I continued to contemplate this and seek the Lord on what this type of worship might look like, I felt quickened by the Lord to turn to Luke 7:36-50. In Luke 7 we read of an account where this very definition of worship is accurately portrayed. Whilst the word worship is never directly mentioned, what we can see very clearly as we read this passage is that the act of worship itself, as defined for us by Jesus, is performed. For our purposes here we will just quote vs 36-38, but please take another pause here and read over Luke 7:36-50.

> *Then one of the Pharisees asked Him to eat with him. And He went to the Pharisee's house, and sat down to eat. And behold, a woman in the city who was a sinner, when she knew that Jesus sat at the table in the Pharisee's house, brought an alabaster flask of fragrant oil, and stood at His feet behind Him weeping; and she began to wash His feet with her tears, and wiped them with the hair of her head; and she kissed His feet and anointed them with the fragrant oil. (Luk 7:36-38)* NKJV

In these verses we are told that Jesus was dining at the house of a Pharisee. While He was there, a woman described as being a sinner had heard where Jesus was and took with her an alabaster box of fragrant oil and went to the Pharisees house. Within these first verses we are presented with two completely opposite ends of the Jewish social classes of the day. We have a Pharisee, holy and religious by the day's standards, and then we have a woman who was a sinner. Whilst we do not know what her sin was, the description indicates that this was a woman living a sinful lifestyle and that this was a fact that was widely known amongst the community. Just as people would have looked on the Pharisee and made an immediate judgement of his holiness, so people would have looked on the woman and made an immediate judgement of her unholiness.

As Jesus was dining, we are told that this woman entered the house. The woman didn't seek the attention of Jesus but stood behind Him. She started to weep and then bent down and started to wash His feet with her tears and dry them with her hair. She then kissed His feet and anointed them with the oil that she had brought with her. All of this happened under the judgemental eyes of the Pharisee and the other guests who were at his house. The woman though, was unperturbed.

What we read here is an amazing encounter of a woman approaching her Saviour. Although the word worship is never directly mentioned, within her actions what we see is the embodiment of the definition of worship that we discovered from our passage in John. We see an individual crouched in a position of adoration at the feet of her King, kissing the feet of her master. The actions of this sinful woman highlight the truths we have already discussed that worship is not just an action, it is also a position and an attitude, literally, physically and spiritually. Truly the act of this sinful woman embodied the truths of the word used by Jesus for worship in John 4, which as a reminder means "to kiss, like a dog licking his master's hand); to fawn or crouch to, i.e. (literally or figuratively) prostrate oneself in homage (do reverence to, adore)". As we read this we see an account that exemplifies the truth that Jesus was communicating about worship.

As we consider the act of the woman kissing and wiping her master's feet, we may be tempted to immediately link that to the thought of a dog licking its master's hand and that this was her worship. And whilst there is truth in that, the kissing and wiping of Jesus feet actually only formed a part of the woman's worship. The wiping and kissing of Jesus feet help us to identify that the woman was worshipping Jesus, but when we take the time to break down and study this encounter, we begin to see that there were actually many individual intrinsic parts which all combine to form the worship that she offered. There are many links in this chain and in order to truly understand the image of worship that we see here, we need to take some time to consider each link and how they individually contribute to the worship that the woman offered. It is as we break down this passage and the actions of this woman, that we gain a greater understanding of what is involved in the worship that Jesus referred to in John 4.

From this example of worship, we learn that:

WORSHIP IS INTENTIONAL.

> *And behold, a woman in the city who was a sinner, when she knew that Jesus sat at the table in the Pharisee's house, brought an alabaster flask of fragrant oil". (Luk 7:37) NKJV*

The worship of the woman didn't happen by accident. It was not by chance or by fluke. She didn't just happen to stumble in to where Jesus was. We are told in Luke that the woman came to know where Jesus was. She somehow heard of Jesus' whereabouts, whether she was intentionally seeking Him or whether she just happened to overhear we don't know. The woman though heard, and she then made a deliberate, conscious choice to go to Him there. It was an intentional action on her behalf. She chose to go to Him. She chose to enter the house. She chose to worship.

The woman was alone. There was no one else with her. There was no one else pushing her forward or coercing her on. This was her choice. There was intent on behalf of the woman. There was a resolve within her that she was going to go and worship her King. There was deliberate, intentional action. How many others also heard where Jesus was? How many others had the exact same opportunity to go unto Him? No one else though chose to! Many would have heard but only one chose to go and worship at the feet of Jesus.

Worship has to be intentional! There must be that resolve within each of us that we are going to worship Him. Regardless of everything else going on, regardless of everyone else around us, we have to choose to intentionally worship Him. No one can make that choice for us. To intentionally come to the King and worship is a choice that we, and we alone, can make.

Worship is Intentional.

WORSHIP REQUIRES PREPARATION.

*"when she knew that Jesus sat at the table in the Pharisee's house, **brought** an alabaster flask of fragrant oil." (Luk 7:37) NKJV*

The woman didn't just find out where Jesus was and go to Him, she took something with her to present unto Him. The woman went prepared for the worship that she would give. Her worship was not an afterthought once she had arrived, but **a pre-thought**. The woman had considered what she would do before she got there. There was intention, but there was also preparation so she could fully follow through on her intent. The woman prepared for what she would do. She went **intentionally** to worship, and she went **prepared** to worship. Both are required!

Such has always been the case with worship. Preparation has always been a necessity for worship. In the Old Testament, the people of Israel never just turned up to worship at the Tabernacle or Temple. They always came prepared to worship. They would select their offerings beforehand and then they would bring these unto the Lord. Their intention was to worship but they had to be prepared before they could! They had to prepare for what they would give.

Worship begins before we ever get to Jesus. Worship is something that involves preparation and when we get to Jesus, we give unto Him that which we have prepared for Him.

Just as the woman prepared before she worshipped Jesus, so to do we. There is preparation that is needed before we get to Jesus and worship.

Worship requires preparation.

WORSHIP IS POSITIONAL.

*"and stood at **His feet** behind Him weeping; and she began to wash His feet with her tears ..."(Luk 7:38) NKJV*

We are told that when the woman was worshipping Jesus, she was found at His feet. Whilst we read that she stood at Jesus feet, the passage then goes on to tell us that she began to wash His feet with her hair. To wash His feet required the woman to change her position. She couldn't stand to do this; she had to kneel which required a change in position. The woman was bowed at the feet of Jesus! Her worship caused her position to change.

The act of bowing before Jesus is one that elevates Him above us. Whilst bowing is a physical act it is also a spiritual declaration of the Kingship of Jesus. It sets Him rightfully above us.

We see this same truth of bowing exemplified a number of times in the book of Revelation.

> *And the four and twenty elders and the four beasts **fell down and worshipped** God that sat on the throne, saying, Amen; Alleluia. (Rev 19:4) KJV*

> *And when he had taken the book, the four beasts and four and twenty **elders fell down** before the Lamb, having every one of them harps, and golden vials full of odours, which are the prayers of saints. (Rev 5:8) KJV*

> *And the four beasts said, Amen. And the four and twenty **elders fell down and worshipped** him that liveth for ever and ever.(Rev 5:14) KJV*

> *See also Rev 7:11, Rev 11:16, Rev 4:10*

Worship involves a reverential fear of who we are worshipping. It is based on an understanding that we are coming before the living God. To bow or kneel before the King, involves a change in our position. It is a **choice** to recognise His authority, His rule, and His majesty. When we understand who we are approaching, bowing becomes a natural position. How can we stand in the presence of the Lord God Almighty?

Worship is Positional.

WORSHIP IS ABOUT HIS GLORY.

> *and stood at His feet behind Him weeping; and she began to wash His feet with her tears,* **and wiped them with the hair of her head**; *and she kissed His feet and anointed them with the fragrant oil. (Luk 7:38) NKJV*

The woman washed His feet with her tears, and then she wiped His feet with the hair of her head. She didn't use a towel or a rag, she used her hair! In 1 Corinthians 11:15 Paul tells us that the long hair of a woman is a glory unto her. Here we see the woman use what was a glory to her, to give glory to the Lord. She used her glory to give Him glory!

Jesus' feet would have been covered in dust and all types of muck from His journeying. They would not have been clean feet that had been protected by socks and shoes. They were feet that were exposed to every element on the roads which He had walked upon. The woman loosened this grit and muck with her tears, but she cleaned it off with her hair. Can you imagine for a moment how dirty her hair would have been from this? One only has to think how dirty a rag gets when washing a muddy car. But a rag wasn't used here, her hair was! That which brought glory to the woman was sacrificed to give glory unto God. The woman didn't give a second thought unto her glory, her focus was on ascribing glory unto the Messiah. That which was her glory was counted as of little value by her as she gave it all unto Him.

Worship at its heart is all about His glory. It is completely and solely about ascribing glory unto Him who is worthy of it. It requires us to let go of those things which would bring us glory and for us to be prepared to bring and sacrifice everything unto Him for His glory. He deserves nothing less!

Worship is about His glory.

WORSHIP IS BASED IN REVERENCE.

> *...and she kissed his feet...(Luke 7:38) NKJV*

The woman bowed at Jesus feet. She washed them, dried them and then she kissed His feet.

In our look at John 4 we discovered how the definition for the word worship used in the Samaritan woman's encounter with Jesus was defined "as a dog licking the master's hand". Here we see the truth of this attitude of worship exemplified. The woman kissed her master's feet. The woman had just cleaned the dirt and muck that would have been on Jesus' feet off with her hair. Then, in an act of complete reverence, she kissed her master's feet. She did not presume to kiss His hands or His face, but his feet. She took the place of ultimate humility and in reverence showered her love upon her Master.

This was not just a singular kiss though; it was a repeated action over and over. As we read further in the account, Jesus in describing the actions of the woman said:

> *You gave Me no kiss, but* ***this woman has not ceased to kiss My feet*** *since the time I came in. (Luk 7:45) NKJV*

From the time that the woman got to Jesus, she did not cease to kiss His feet. This was not a ceremonial act to give benevolence to someone, this was not a couple of kisses, this was a continual act of reverential worship. She kissed and kissed and kissed her master's feet. Just as a dog continues to lick the master's hand, so the woman continually kissed the feet of her master.

The woman knew who she was, but she also knew who Jesus was. She understood the gap between the two of them and as such she approached her Messiah accordingly. Her worship was based in reverence of who Jesus is.

Worship is based in reverence.

WORSHIP IS SACRIFICIAL.

> *...brought an alabaster flask of fragrant oil, ... and anointed them (Jesus feet) with the fragrant oil. (Luk 7:37-38) NKJV*

The Greek word for ointment as used here is defined by Strongs as "myrhh, that is (by implication) perfumed oil". The woman anointed the feet of Jesus with perfumed oil.

The perfumed oil was something that would had a cost and normally the intended use of this perfumed oil would have been on self. From scripture we do not know whether the woman bought it specifically for Jesus on her way to the pharisees house or whether this was something that she had previously bought for herself and now wanted to sacrifice unto Jesus. Whichever was the case, using this perfumed oil to anoint the feet of Jesus cost the woman. There was an expense to what she did. It was a sacrificial act. The woman took something which was valuable, and she choose to give that unto Jesus. She chose to deny herself the blessing of the perfumed oil and instead chose to lavish upon the Lord that which was valuable to her. She sacrificed that which would have benefited her and given her pleasure. She chose to sacrificially offer this fragrance unto Jesus. She chose to pour it out upon Him, despite knowing how it could have blessed her.

The first mention of a word in scripture is always significant. In the King James Translation of the Bible the first time that the word worship is specifically used is in connection with Abraham offering Isaac as a sacrifice unto the Lord in worship.

> *And Abraham said to his young men, "Stay here with the donkey; the lad and I will go yonder and **worship**, and we will come back to you." (Gen 22:5) NKJV*

Abraham was called to sacrificial worship that had a cost! The first time that the word worship is used we see that it is unequivocally and undeniably linked to sacrifice!

The truth is, worship always involves the people of God giving something unto God sacrificially. I would go as far as to say that without sacrifice there can be no true worship. David sums up this sentiment in 2 Samuel 24:24:

> *Then the king said to Araunah, "No, but I will surely buy it from you for a price; **nor will I offer burnt offerings to the LORD my God with that which costs me nothing.**" So David bought the threshing floor and the oxen for fifty shekels of silver. (2Sa 24:24) NKJV*

When the prophet Gad declared to King David that he was to go and erect an altar to the Lord at the threshing floor of Araunah the Jebusite, David refused to accept the threshing floor from Araunah as a gift. He insisted upon paying for it even though as king, he had every right to just take possession of it and claim it as his own. David though understood that worship always involves a cost. If there is no cost to give something, then by nature it is not sacrificial. When we give something that doesn't affect us in any way it is in reality charity. We give, or rather donate, to charity things that we no longer use or have need for and are generally not of any cost to us. These are things that are generally quite insignificant to us. Worship cannot be like that! God does not deserve our charity! He deserves infinitely more than that.

Worship by its very nature involves a cost. We cannot offer to God something that costs us nothing. Worship is sacrificial by nature. We are to worship like David when we come before the Lord and be prepared to give of ourselves. We need to have an attitude that refuses to offer anything to God that doesn't cost us.

Worship involves sacrifice.

WORSHIPS PLACES AND KEEPS JESUS AT THE FOREFRONT.

> *And stood at his feet behind him weeping, ……(Luk 7:38)*
> NKJV

From the description that we are given in Luke, the woman was bowed at the feet of Jesus, but she was behind Him and He was in front of her. She was behind, Jesus was in front.

Worship, whether it is private or corporate, always puts and keeps Jesus at the forefront. Worship always exalts Jesus to the position of pre-eminence and prominence. It uplifts and places Him front and centre. In worship we assume our place, kneeled behind, so that He can assume His rightful place, uplifted and in front.

In Psalm 22 we read:

> *But thou art holy, O thou that inhabitest the praises of Israel.*
> *(Psa 22:3) KJV*

According to Strongs the Hebrew word for 'inhabitest', as used above, is defined as "to sit down (specifically as judge, in ambush, in quiet); by implication to dwell, to remain; causatively to settle, to marry".

This word is used extensively in scripture and the majority of times it is translated as dwell/dwelt, inhabits, sit/sat. It has the connotation of dwelling and sitting. In other Biblical translations this verse is translated as 'the Lord is enthroned on the praises of Israel'. The Lord dwells enthroned (seated), upon the praises of His people. When we praise, the Lord comes in amongst those that are praising Him. Our worship invites Him in as we give Him the pre-eminence and prominence He deserves.

When we worship and praise, it brings in a fresh focus of His kingship in our lives, congregations etc. It is an act that puts Him front and centre for that is where He belongs. A King doesn't rule from the back of the room! The King rules at the front and that is where He is to remain. He is the focus always. There should be nothing that gets in the way of the King being enthroned front and centre.

Worship puts and keeps Jesus at the forefront.

WORSHIP IS DONE IN FAITH.

> *Then He (Jesus) said to the woman, "Your faith has saved you.*
> *Go in peace." (Luk 7:50) NKJV*

Throughout this encounter we read that the Pharisee spoke, Jesus spoke and those who were at the table spoke. A lot of people had a lot of things to say! The one person that never said a word in this account though is the woman. She did not utter a word and yet Jesus told her that her sins were forgiven because **her faith** had saved her. Jesus credited the faith of the woman as the reason for her saving. This was a faith that was evidenced despite the woman never uttering a word!

The actions of the woman were actions of faith. In faith the woman sought Jesus. In faith she brought perfumed oil with her. In faith she wept at His feet. In faith she wiped His feet. In faith she kissed His feet. In faith she anointed His feet. The worship of the woman was done completely and totally in faith. It was through her faith filled actions that she declared who Jesus was to her and to all those around her. Her faith, though internal, had an external manifestation that was evident to all who looked upon her. It was her faith that brought her to Jesus and her faith that saw her worship Him despite her past and despite those in whose presence she worshipped.

The faith of the woman to pursue Jesus here should not be underestimated. She would have known how she would have been received at the house of a pharisee, and she would have heard and been well aware of the comments floating around from the other dinner party guests as she worshipped. Despite all this, the faith of the woman dictated her actions. Her path was not swayed, and it was her steadfast faith that Jesus commended her for. Her worship and her faith went hand in hand. She had a holy, reverential fear that elicited a response of faith in her actions.

Worship is done in faith.

WORSHIP STEMS FROM LOVE.

> *"There was a certain creditor who had two debtors. One owed five hundred denarii, and the other fifty. And when they had nothing with which to repay, he freely forgave them both. Tell Me, therefore, which of them will **love** him more?" Simon answered and said, "I suppose the one whom he forgave more." And He said to him, "You have rightly judged."*
>
> *Therefore I say to you, her sins, which are many, are forgiven, for **she loved much**. But to whom little is forgiven, the same **loves little**." (Luk 7:41-43, 47) NKJV*

Worship flows from the love that we have in our hearts for the Lord. In this account Jesus used a parable to explain to the pharisee the difference between the love of the woman and the love of the pharisees.

One of the greatest hindrances to any worship is religious piousness. The pharisees held themselves as the benchmark of religious obedience and would have considered their need for forgiveness as negligible. They considered themselves righteous by their own standards and would have thought that they had little need of a saviour. The woman though recognised exactly who Jesus was and the gap that existed between her and Him. She understood the level of forgiveness she needed, and she loved much.

The reality is that all have sinned and fallen short of the glory of God. No one is perfect. Between each and every one of us and God exists a gap which only Jesus can bridge. When we individually have a proper understanding of where our lives would be without the intervention of Jesus it should stir such a depth of love in us that our actions should mirror the woman's. When we truly understand all that He has done for us, it cannot but stir a love in us that leads us to worship.

Worship stems from love.

WORSHIP IS FOCUSED ON HIM NOT SELF.

> *And behold, a woman in the city who was a sinner, when she knew that Jesus sat at the table in the Pharisee's house, brought an alabaster flask of fragrant oil,"* (Luk 7:37) NKJV

The woman is openly described as a sinner by Luke. Her life and her lifestyle must have been one that did not align with the commandments of God. The woman's standing with God was openly known.

The woman could have let feelings of shame, inadequacy and worthlessness stop her from seeking Jesus out and going to the pharisee's house. No doubt the enemy threw these accusations at her mind as she approached. We can all probably imagine what thoughts the enemy might have thrown her way: "You're going to go where? You are going to do what? You think you will be accepted?" The woman though did not let her sin hinder her, she let it propel her towards the only one who could forgive it.

The woman understood who she was and her need for the forgiveness of her Lord. Rather than be dictated to by a focus on self though, she chose to focus in on Him. The woman didn't focus in on the truth of who she was. She focused in on the truth of who He was and the need she had of Him. Worship removes any focus on self and solely focuses in on Him. In worship we cannot be both self-focused and God focused. We can only be one or the other. The woman chose to be God focused.

Worship chooses to focus in on Him. It switches off the distractions of self and the enemy and focuses its gaze solely on the living God.

Worship is focused on Him not self.

WORSHIP IS FOCUSED ON HIM NOT PEOPLE.

> *Now when the Pharisee who had invited Him saw this, he spoke to himself, saying, "This Man, if He were a prophet, would know who and what manner of woman this is who is touching Him, for she is a sinner." (Luk 7:39) NKJV*

The woman knew who she was and the life she had lived. She would have also been well aware of the fact that everyone else also knew the type of woman that she was and the life she had lived. Everyone in that room would have known the woman and looked down on her. She would have stood out like a sore thumb, and she would have felt the weight of the judgmental stares aimed at her.

The woman not only went to the house of the pharisee knowing what type of reception she would receive; she remained there whilst no doubt being judged and having snide comments about her thrown around the room. The woman though chose not to focus on those that were there or their thoughts about her, but rather she focused her attention solely upon Jesus.

Just as worship cannot be both self-focused and God focused, neither can it be focused on others and focused on God! Because in reality a focus on the thoughts of others and what they think of us is in reality just another form of self-focus. The worship we give cannot be dictated by what we think others will think of us. It has got to be completely and solely God focused. Again, it is one or the other.

As the woman worshipped, her focus was solely on who Jesus was. He was the reason she worshipped. Nothing else mattered and nothing else consumed her focus. She didn't care what others thought, she didn't care what others were saying, because her focus was not there. She was completely focused on Jesus, not on the others in the room.

Worship is focused on Him not people.

WORSHIP IS BASED IN HUMILITY.

> *"And stood at His feet behind Him weeping; and she began to wash His feet with her tears, and wiped them with the hair of her head; and she kissed His feet and anointed them with the fragrant oil". (Luk 7:38) NKJV*

What we read here tells us that the woman was first washing the feet of Jesus before she kissed them and then anointed them. To wash someone's feet was a demeaning job. In our earlier point, **'Worship is about His glory'**, we noted how the feet of a person living in Biblical times would have been covered in dirt, mud and muck from their travels. To wash this off was not the role of a master, but of a servant. It was a base job and to be asked to do this for someone would have been demeaning.

To intentionally choose to wash someone's feet was an ultimate act of humility. The truth of this is seen when Jesus washed his disciples' feet. For Jesus to wash His disciples' feet made absolutely no natural sense. He was their master, and they His servants. Such was the counter intuitiveness of this that Simon Peter resisted Jesus washing his feet. The message of Jesus through this act though was that if He, their master and Lord, was prepared to humble Himself and undertake this undignified, humble and demeaning role in serving them, they too should serve one another in the same manner.

By washing the feet of Jesus, the woman showed that she was not concerned or worried about what He had walked in. She came and chose a position of humility before her Saviour. She abased herself and in humility, with no thought of personal pride, worshipped her King. No other guest in that room was prepared to humble themselves and do what she did! The woman though in humility, worshipped her King without a second thought.

Worship is based in humility.

WORSHIP IS NOT FOCUSED ON TIME.

> *You gave Me no kiss, but this woman has not ceased to kiss My feet* **since the time I came in.** *(Luk 7:45) NKJV*

Compare the differences here as highlighted by Jesus. Simon the pharisee didn't have the time or didn't make the time to welcome Jesus with a kiss when He arrived, the woman though from the time that she arrived did not stop kissing the feet of Jesus. We are not told how long Jesus had been there, but the fact that Jesus mentions the extended duration of the woman's worship shows that it must have been for a substantial period of time.

This was not a quick act of the woman and nor was it one that was focused on the clock so that she would know when she could stop. The worship of the woman had absolutely no focus on time because her focus was on the eternal! The woman's duration of worship was not dictated to by the things of this world. Her worship was absolutely pure. There was no schedule to stick to, no other tasks to interrupt it, no other distractions. Her worship was completely and solely focused on adoring her Lord.

Worship is not focused on time.

WORSHIP RECOGNISES WHO HE IS.

> *"And stood at His feet behind Him weeping; and she began to wash His feet with her tears, and wiped them with the hair of her head; and she kissed His feet and anointed them with the fragrant oil." (Luk 7:37-38) NKJV*

The woman heard that Jesus was at the pharisee's house and went unto Him there. As has been already said, the pharisees were the benchmark of religion in those days. They were the holy ones, the ones esteemed as the religious elite. We are also told that it was not just Simon and Jesus at the house, there were other guests as well. No doubt these other guests were most likely other pharisees and religious leaders. These were the kind of people that Simon would have associated with, those of a similar class.

So, within the house there were many religious and dignified people and yet despite all of this, the only feet that the woman washed were those of Jesus. The woman did not wash the feet of any of the pharisees! She did not wash the feet of any of the other guests there. Her worship was focused on Jesus and Him alone.

Worship recognises who He is and that He alone is worthy of our worship. Worship does not get caught up or focused on anything else going on in the room or anyone else that is in the room. True worship is focused solely on Him.

Worship recognises who He is.

WORSHIP IN TRANSFIXED ON HIM.

> *And behold, a woman in the city who was a sinner, when she knew that Jesus sat at the table in the Pharisee's house, brought an alabaster flask of fragrant oil,* **and stood at His feet** *behind Him weeping; and she began to wash His feet with her tears, and wiped them with the hair of her head; and she kissed His feet and anointed them with the fragrant oil. (Luk 7:37-38) NKJV*

The woman interrupted a dinner party. There would have been people eating, conversations going on, possibly people serving food. There would have been noise and distractions everywhere and yet the woman's worship never deviated. Nothing distracted her from giving her worship unto Jesus.

Worship recognises exactly who He is and that He alone is worthy of our worship. When we are transfixed on Him in worship, as we should be, everything else fades away. Nothing else matters, because we recognise just who we are in the presence of. All of the external noise fades away, as our focus in completely transfixed on Him.

Worship is transfixed on Him alone.

WORSHIP CHANGES THE ATMOSPHERE.

> *And behold, a woman in the city who was a sinner, when she knew that Jesus sat at the table in the Pharisee's house,* **brought an alabaster flask of fragrant oil**, *and stood at His feet behind Him weeping; and she began to wash His feet with her tears, and wiped them with the hair of her head; and she kissed His feet and* **anointed them with the fragrant oil.**
> (Luk 7:37-38) NKJV

When the woman came and worshipped at the feet of Jesus, we are told that she broke open the alabaster flask of perfume that she had with her. As part of her worship, she proceeded to anoint Jesus' feet with the oil. When that jar was broken open, its fragrance would have permeated the whole room. This was not just a spray or a drop of perfume that she applied. She opened the jar and anointed the feet of her King. There would have been a discernible change in the environment because of the worship that was occurring. The sweet-smelling aroma would have wafted out and filled the whole room and house. All who were present would have been able to smell that which had been offered. One can almost imagine the image of all those present slowly noticing the aroma and turning to look for where it was originating from. There would have been a change in the atmosphere that couldn't have been denied. The worship of the woman changed the fragrance of the room.

So often in worship we look for the internal proofs that the presence of God has turned up. We look for what we have felt on the inside and that is often our plumbline for judging worship. But what we see here is that worship, in a corporate setting, is something that should impact the atmosphere of the whole room. Whilst the woman was worshiping Jesus individually, she was doing it in a public or corporate setting. What we see is that the actions of an individual in worship impacted the area around them. What was offered caused a shift that was able to be noticed by all. The worship that was given changed the fragrance of the room. There was a change that none could deny. Whilst not everyone was worshipping and possibly not everyone enjoyed the smell, all would have been able to smell the change in the aroma of the room.

Worship changes the atmosphere. It has an external impact that is tangible. Worship is a sweet-smelling incense that should permeate our corporate settings. It should provide an aroma that all who are in the room can discern. It is not something that we can create or have a recipe for but is a naturally occurring result of true worship.

Worship changes the atmosphere.

WORSHIP IS NOT DEPENDENT ON MUSIC.

Throughout the whole account of the woman worshipping Jesus we see that what she did was essentially done in silence. She did not speak, there was no music or signing and yet we unequivocally see an act of worship. As the woman knelt there quietly sobbing, wiping and kissing Jesus' feet her actions spoke far louder than any words or musical chords every could.

Worship in itself is not dependant on music, it is actually something that stems from within an individual. The worship of the woman stemmed from the faith and love that was within her. Worship starts in the heart and whilst music and singing may aid us in helping to release that, our worship is not dependent upon either of them. Like the woman, sometimes our worship needs to be done in the stillness and quietness of His presence.

In looking at this account of the woman who anointed the feet of Jesus we have discovered a number of points that define what worship looks like. As a reminder our purpose in doing this was to gain insight into the word for worship that Jesus used in His account with the Samaritan woman. As we looked at the Greek definition, we discovered that the word for worship used by Jesus meant "to kiss, like a dog licking his master's hand); to fawn or crouch to, i.e. (literally or figuratively) prostrate oneself in homage (do reverence to, adore)."

It is in this example of the woman who anointed the feet of Jesus that we see the very embodiment of this definition of worship that Jesus referred to. We see that image of a dog in humble submission before its master, adoring and loving Him. This account of the sinful woman actually shows us what our worship is to look like. It sets for us an example of the worship that Jesus deserves. The woman was a living example of the worship that Jesus spoke of to the Samaritan woman at the well. She was a worshipper.

Summary

In this section we have seen that within Jesus' conversation with the Samaritan woman there was an undeniable focus on worship. Whilst the Samaritan woman introduced the topic, it was Jesus who focused in intently on worship and revealed the true worship that the Father is seeking.

As we have sought to gain an insight into Jesus' words here, we discovered that worship, as used in this passage, has a definition we do not usually associate with worship or perhaps one that we are uncomfortable with. It is a humbling act, one in which we need to understand the servant master relationship. It is a definition that illustrates the adoration, love and submission we are to have towards our Lord. The definition of a dog licking its master's hand can seem degrading to us. The reality though is that to see a dog licking its master's hand is quite natural. The dog recognises their master's position, and its licking is in recognition of that. Now if a dog can naturally recognise the authority of their natural master, it should not seem so absurd for us to be able to recognise the authority of our spiritual master. The act of licking does not debase the dog. We do not think any less of a dog for doing this. Quite the opposite, we immediately recognise the love and affection that the animal has for its master. So too is it with worship. Worship does not debase us. Worship shows the love and affection that we have for our master. It should be a natural occurrence.

The example of the woman anointing Jesus' feet in Luke 7 perfectly illustrates this truth. No true believer reads that account and thinks less of the woman. As we read the account we should see an act of worship that inspires us to go deeper in our own! The woman's act of worship is one that our own worship should mirror. That same worship should flow from each and every follower of Christ as our normal response in recognition of who He is. This type of worship is the worship that Jesus spoke about to the Samaritan woman. We are called to be worshippers, and the focus is never on us abasing ourselves but rather it is always on magnifying Him. Throughout every aspect of the woman's worship her focus was unwavering. As we examined the actions of the sinful woman, we learned that worship, as defined by Jesus to the Samaritan woman, has the following aspects:

- Worship is intentional.
- Worship requires preparation.
- Worship is positional.
- Worship is about His glory.
- Worship is based in reverence.
- Worship is sacrificial.
- Worship places and keeps Jesus at the forefront.
- Worship is done in faith.
- Worship stems from love.
- Worship is focused on Him not self.

- Worship is focused on Him not others.
- Worship is based in humility.
- Worship is not focused on time.
- Worship recognises who He is.
- Worship is transfixed on Him.
- Worship changes the atmosphere.
- Worship is not dependent on music.

This is the worship that the sinful woman offered, and we as believers are called to the same standard.

We have looked here at what worship is in the context of John 4. The actions of the sinful woman have revealed to us the worship that Jesus spoke of. But the words of Jesus in John 4 are deeper than first glance. Whilst Jesus calls us to worship, He also sets a qualification for what true worship is. The words of Jesus are that true worshippers will worship the Father in spirit and in truth. So, in order to fulfill this call of Jesus call to worship, we need to offer the kind of worship exemplified by the sinful woman at Jesus feet, but we are to do this **IN SPIRIT AND IN TRUTH**. We are not to just replicate her actions, but we are to offer the kind of worship that she demonstrated in spirit and in truth. It is when we do that that we offer true worship, the true worship that the Father is seeking.

In other words, there are qualifiers for worship to be considered true. Worship cannot be an act that we mirror or replicate. Whilst there are characteristics that should align in our worship with that of the woman's example, the true worship that we are called to offer needs to be in spirit and in truth. We are to follow the sinful woman's example, but we are to do so in spirit and in truth. The question now becomes, what does this mean and how do we do it? These are things that we will consider in our next section.

Having gained an understanding of what worship looks like, we now turn out attention to what it means to offer true worship in spirit and in truth.

The Standard of True

> *But the hour is coming, and now is, when the true worshipers will worship the Father in spirit and truth; for the Father is seeking such to worship Him. God is Spirit, and those who worship Him must worship in spirit and truth." (Joh 4:23-24) NKJV*

Having gained an understanding of what Jesus meant by worship, we now turn our focus back to Jesus' encounter with the Samaritan woman and specifically on what He said in verses 23 and 24 of John 4. Whilst this is a small passage within the context of the conversation, within it is a vast amount of truth for us to grasp hold of. This passage provides us with three key aspects that Jesus gives in regard to true worship. These are: a definition of true worship, an encouragement for true worship and finally a call to true worship.

THE DEFINITION OF TRUE WORSHIP.

> ***true worshippers*** *will worship the Father* ***in spirit*** *and* ***in truth*** *(Joh 4:23) NKJV*

The first thing that we see is that Jesus defined what true worship is. As a quick recap the woman had been talking about Samaritan worshippers and Jewish worshippers. Jesus though, set aside these distinct and divided groups and introduced a new group, **TRUE WORSHIPPERS**. In doing this, Jesus defined for us what true worship looks like. Whilst the Jews and the Samaritans had been divided in their worship because of their focus on the place where worship was performed, this new group, true worshippers, would not be focused on the place of worship but rather on the approach of worship. The true worship that these true worshippers would offer unto the Father would be in spirit and in truth.

True worship is worship that is done in spirit and in truth.

THE ENCOURAGEMENT FOR TRUE WORSHIP.

*The Father is **seeking** such to worship Him. (Joh 4:23)*
NKJV

After Jesus defined what true worship is, He then went on to say that the Father is seeking this kind of worshipper. The Greek word used here is 'Zeteo' and carries with it the thought of not only looking for but the sense of desiring for and a requiring of. The Father is not just looking for this type of worshipper, it is also a standard He requires and is one He is desiring His people to reach. Our heavenly Father is actively looking for this type of worshipper.

In this statement, Jesus again seeks to set aside the Samaritans woman's understanding of worship. His goal is to take the attention off what man thinks of worship, be they Jew or Samaritan, and to cause the focus to shift to what God thinks about worship. This is an encouragement not just for the Samaritan woman, but for all believers to be the kind of worshipper that the Father is seeking.

The Father is seeking true worshippers who worship in spirit and in truth.

THE CALL TO TRUE WORSHIP.

*Those who worship **must** worship in spirt an in truth (Joh 4:24) NKJV*

Jesus has defined true worship, He has stated that this is the kind of worship that the Father is seeking and now He takes things one step further by telling the Samaritan woman that they who worship the Lord

MUST worship in spirit and in truth. In other words, this is not a suggestion or an alternative approach, but rather this is the standard that the Lord requires. Jesus in essence was saying to the woman that it didn't matter about how the Jews worshipped or about how the Samaritans worshipped, anyone who worships the Father must do it according to the Father's standard, in spirit and in truth.

The Greek word used for 'must' here is the word 'dei', and according to Strongs it means, "it is necessary (as binding)". This word does not imply a casual suggestion by Jesus, but rather a requirement of the Lord that rests upon His people. This is how worship **MUST** be done.

Jesus here lifted the focus of the woman. He was growing her understanding and in doing so He was setting the standard of what true worship is. He essentially said to woman, "if you are sincere in your desire to worship the Lord, then this is how it must be done! Forget man's standards, this is God's standard!"

We are called to be true worshippers who worship the Father in spirit and in truth.

In these two verses, Jesus laid out a qualification for what true worship is and outlined for us what true worship is comprised of. In order for there to be true worship it must be worship that is done in spirit and truth. We will refer to this as 'The Standard of True', and we can simplify it to be expressed as:

Worship In Spirit + Worship In Truth = True Worship

True worship is made up of both of these factors. On two occasions between John 4:23-24 Jesus outlined the necessity of these qualifications. True worship is not just any type of worship, it is not something that man can set the standards for. The standard for true worship is set by the Lord and it consists of worship that is in spirit and worship that is in truth. The Father is seeking this type of worship from his children, and this is how those that worship the Father **must** worship Him.

> *God is Spirit, and those who worship Him **must worship** in spirit and truth." (Joh 4:24) NKJV*

This is not the type of worship that the Father would like us to aspire to one day, this is the necessary worship that the people of God must offer if they truly want to worship the Father. This is not an option for worship on the behalf of man, it is Gods directed prescription for what true worship is. True worship must be done according to Gods standard.

As I contemplated this standard and sought to define these two elements and how they equated to true worship, I was struck by the implication that if there is a standard for true worship and worship that meets this standard, then there is also worship that doesn't meet the standard of true. The fact that there is true worship indicates that there is worship that is not true. This is the essence of what Jesus was saying when He spoke with the Samaritan woman, attempting to lift her understanding of what worship actually is. He was explaining to her that there is worship that doesn't meet the Lord's standards and then there is the kind of worship, true worship, that the Father is seeking.

Not True or False?

The danger we can have in looking at the standard of true worship and what it involves, is that we can be tempted to jump to the conclusion that that which doesn't equal true worship would be the opposite of true worship, i.e. false worship. In other words, we can think that if our worship isn't in spirit and in truth then it is not true worship but false worship. We would take the equation above and adapt it to read:

$$\text{Worship } \underline{\text{Not}} \text{ In Spirit} + \text{Worship } \underline{\text{Not}} \text{ In Truth} = \text{False Worship}$$

In our natural minds if something isn't true then by necessity it is false. It is something that is black or white, it is either one or the other. The more that I contemplated this thought though, the more I felt that in this case we are not dealing with opposites. We are not dealing with black and white or one or the other. The interaction between the Samaritan woman and Jesus was centred around worship with Jesus expounding to her the truth of worship. What we read of in these verses is of a Godly standard that the Lord is encouraging His people to attain to. The Lord is wanting His people to be true worshippers, in fact He is seeking them to be such, and He has set the standards by which this occurs. God has set the benchmark of what true worship is. Anything that falls short of this, is not false worship, **but** it is worship that falls short of the Lord's standard and therefore isn't the true worship that the Father is seeking. It is not false worship, but nor is it worship that meets the standard of true.

To expand this thought a little further, let us for a moment consider false worship from a Biblical perspective. False worship is something that may have a guise of godliness, but at its core it doesn't worship or glorify the Lord at all. Just as true worship worships the true God, false worship worships a false god! We can see examples of this when Aaron made the Golden Calf shortly after the exodus from Egypt and when Jeroboam made two golden calves for Israel to worship shortly after the kingdom of Israel was divided in two. In both instances we read that the people of Israel came to these idols to worship their 'god', and in both instances they were not worshipping the Lord but a false god that they had created! This was false worship of an idol. We see more examples of false worship with the people of Israel and the nations that surrounded them throughout the Bible. We see the worship of Baal by the people of Israel in the time of Elijah (1 Kings 18), we read of the Philistines temples to their god Dagon when the Ark of the covenant was captured (1 Sam 5) and in the New Testament we read of the goddess Diana worshipped by the people of Ephesus (Acts 19:21-41). All of these are examples of false worship. There is nothing God glorifying in false worship as it is the worship of a false god! False worship is the opposite of what true worship is.

If we look further into this theme of false, we see in scripture accounts of false Christs and false prophets, who have a form of godliness, but their actual motives are to cause the people of God to be deceived and to rebel against the Lord (Mat 24:11 & 24, Jer 14:14, 23:32, Deut 13). False worship, false prophets, false teachers etc are all the opposite of Godly ordained ways and offices, the complete opposite. None of these things that are associated as being false bring any glory unto the Lord. They may have the appearance of being similar, but anything that is false is in fact counter to God. You cannot falsely worship the true God!

But that is not what we are dealing with in John 4. We are not dealing with the opposite of true worship. I would suggest that this verse in John is not setting true worship against false worship, but rather it is setting the standard of true worship for which all believers must aim. Jesus was setting the benchmark of what true worship is. If we do not meet it, we are not false worshippers, but we are falling short of the mark that the Lord has set for true worship.

God has revealed to us the standard for true worship, and it is one which we should be moving toward. If we are not there, it does not mean our worship is false, it just reveals that our worship requires **GROWTH**. This is not a condemnation, but rather an encouragement that should be enough to spur every believer on to offer unto the Lord the worship that the Father is seeking. The heart of every believer should always be to offer unto the Lord true worship for He deserves nothing less! It is something that the Lord has laid out for us and if we are not reaching that standard, we need to look at and adjust our approach.

As believers we need to understand that in worship there is a standard for true worship. The Father is looking for true worshippers! He is actively seeking this from His people. The Father is looking, wanting, desiring the true worship of His people. Knowing this should create a fire and passion within each of us to make sure that this is a standard we reach.

Whilst we have discovered that Gods standard of true worship is:

Worship In Spirit + Worship In Truth = True Worship

What we can now also see is that worship that falls short of this is not false worship. It is still worship of the Father, but it does not equal true worship:

Worship **Not** In Spirit + Worship **Not** In Truth ≠ True Worship

Whilst there is a standard for true worship, any worship that falls short of this means that the worship we offer does not equal true worship. It is not false worship, but neither is it true worship. It falls short of the standard that the Lord has set. From the above equations we can see that whether or not our worship meets Gods standard of true is determined by whether the worship that we offer is **'in spirit' or 'not in spirit'** and whether we offer it **'in truth' or 'not in truth'**.

In order for us to fully understand this standard of true worship, we must understand the differences between the two constants required for true worship. That is, we need to know the difference between our worship being in spirit or not in spirit and the differences between our worship being in truth or not in truth. In taking time to consider these we will build an understanding of what separates worship that falls short of Gods standard from worship that meets His standards. These are points that we will explore in more detail further in the study, but I will endeavour to provide enough information here to briefly explain my thought process.

Worship in Spirit OR Not in Spirit

The first constant that we see for true worship is that it must be done in spirit. But what does that mean? What does it mean to worship in spirit and similarly what does it mean to not worship in spirit? What I would suggest is that in order to worship in spirit we need to have a focus on the Spirit, the Holy Spirit. To worship in spirit is to be Spirit minded and have our focus on the things of God. Here we are not so much talking about the characteristics of worship, but rather where our focus is. Worship in spirit has its focus on the Spirit.

Throughout the Word of God, we see time and time again that which opposes the Spirit is the flesh. The Spirit and the flesh stand counter to one another and when we are not worshipping in Spirit, our focus is actually on the flesh. In this instance we do see that the law of opposite applies. Worship that is not in Spirit is actually worship in the flesh.

Paul in Galatians 5 tells us that the flesh and the Spirit war against each other within us, they compete against one another.

> *I say then: Walk in the **Spirit**, and you shall not fulfill the lust of the **flesh**. For the **flesh** lusts against the **Spirit**, and the **Spirit** against the **flesh**; and these are contrary to one another, so that you do not do the things that you wish. (Gal 5:16-17)*
> NKJV

In these verses Paul explains that it is one or the other. The flesh and the Spirit are contrary to each other. If we walk in the Spirit, we won't fulfill the lusts of the flesh but if we walk in the flesh we won't fulfil the desires of the Spirit. The crux of Paul's message is that we can't walk in both at the same time as they are contrary to each other. They war against each other, each trying to pull us in a particular direction, either to the Spirit or to the flesh.

In worship we see this same pull between the Spirit and the flesh. If we think of a tug of war rope, there are two opposing ends that pull against each other. They are in opposition. In the very middle of the rope is a mark or a ribbon. This ribbon is the goal of the opposing ends. As they pull against each other, they fight to bring the centre ribbon over to their side and claim the victory. In applying this analogy to worship we would say that the focus of worship itself is the centre ribbon on the rope. At one end of the rope, we have the flesh and at the other end of the rope we have the Spirit. These two pull against each other, fighting for the focus in worship. The Spirit and the flesh are literally opposite ends of the rope.

True worship requires our focus to be 100% on the Spirit. There can be no mixture within us. It can't be 70/30 or 50/50. Our focus must be completely and solely on the Spirit. For when our focus is there, our focus is completely on Him and completely removed from off ourselves. Flesh seeks to keep a focus on itself, and this has no place in worship.

The difference here is seen in the focus of our worship. In order to worship in spirit our focus needs to be on the Spirit side. If our focus is on the flesh though, it means that our worship is not worship in spirit.

In true worship we need to have a right focus on the Spirit.

Worship in Truth OR Not in Truth

Again, we may ask what does Jesus mean by worship in truth? And what does it mean to not worship in truth? What separates worship that meets the standard of true from that which doesn't?

Jesus tells us in the gospel of John:

> *Sanctify them by Your truth.* ***Your word is truth****. (Joh 17:17) NKJV*

To worship in truth is to worship according to the truth of worship that the Lord has outlined within the Word of God. It cannot be in presumption, or according to our desires, it must be according to God's divine standard. To worship in truth is to worship in the right way, Gods way. To not worship in truth is to worship in a way that does not completely align with the approach that God has outlined through His Word.

On the opposite side of this, to **NOT** worship in truth is actually to worship in error. This may seem out of place to have error as the opposite of truth as it would no doubt seem more fitting for lie to be the opposite of truth. As I was considering this though, I was prompted that worship is never done in a lie. A lie is a distortion of the truth which leads man to error. Causing the people of God to err through the provision of a lie is one of Satan's oldest tricks. This is what happened with Adam and Eve. In the Garden of Eden, the serpent **TWISTED** the truth of God's Word, the woman **BELIEVED** the lie and both she and Adam ended up in **ERROR**. They erred having believed the lie. In terms of worship, the same thing happens when we get deceived by a lie, we step out of line with the truth, and we end up worshipping in error. When we don't worship in truth, we worship in error.

We see these opposites confirmed by the Apostle John.

> *We are of God. He who knows God hears us; he who is not of God does not hear us. By this we know the* **spirit of truth** *and the* **spirit of error.** *(1Jn 4:6) NKJV*

As believers, I would suggest that we don't choose to worship a lie, but we can be deceived by a lie to worship in error. It is not truth vs lie, but rather truth vs error. The difference between truth and error is seen in the way we worship. If we are to worship in truth, then we need to worship in the right way according to the truths of God's word. If we are not worshipping in the right way, we are in fact worshipping in error, having been deceived by a lie and deviated from the path of truth. As the people of God our true worship must be done in truth and according to the truth.

We will expand on each of these thoughts in the proceeding sections, but sufficient information has been given here to briefly explain my thought process. It is with an understanding of these points, though brief to date, that we start to gain a greater insight into Gods standard of true worship.

True Worship

With the information we have discovered we can now update our initial equation from the start of this section. If we apply this new information from what we have learned above, we see now see that the standard for true worship looks like:

$$\underset{\text{(Right focus)}}{\text{Worship In Spirit}} + \underset{\text{(Right way)}}{\text{Worship In Truth}} = \text{True Worship}$$

We can also now update our equation for worship that doesn't meet the standard of true. As we have discovered worship not in spirit is actually worship in flesh and comes from having a wrong focus in worship. Similarly worship not in truth is actually worship in error and comes from being deceived to worship in a way that does not align with the truths of the Word. Worship in the flesh (wrong focus) and worship in error (wrong way) do not equal true worship. With this understanding we can update our second equation of **worship not in spirit** and **worship not in truth** to now read:

$$\text{Worship In Flesh (Wrong Focus)} + \text{Worship In Error (Wrong Way)} \neq \text{True Worship}$$

This worship isn't false worship, as we have discussed, but it is worship that does not meet the standard of true worship that the Lord has set. It is not the worship that the Father is seeking, and it is not what we are called to offer! It falls short of the divine standard.

The fact that Jesus sets the benchmark for true worship, shows us that there is worship that doesn't attain to this standard. Whilst Jesus outlines what true worship is, through His definition we can also glean what true worship isn't.

TRUE WORSHIP	**NOT TRUE WORSHIP**
Worship in Spirit. *(Right Focus)*	Worship in Flesh. *(Wrong Focus)*
Worship in Truth. *(Right Way)*	Worship in Error. *(Wrong Way)*

Such seems a very simple definition of what we are and aren't to do, and if that was all there was our approach would seem rather straight forward. There is actually more to this though! The reality is that this is not the end of the equation. It is not just one approach versus the other. The truth of this is rather more challenging for us as believers.

If we look back to the standard of true, there are actually **two** conditions that have to be met in order for worship to be considered true. That is,

THE STANDARD OF TRUE

both of the conditions have to exist at the same time in order for worship to be true and for it to be the kind of worship that the Father is seeking. If we return to our original equation what we actually see is that:

$$\text{Worship In Spirit} + \text{Worship In Truth} = \text{True Worship}$$

Notice the **'PLUS'** sign. It takes both of these conditions to be met in order for worship to be true. Jesus didn't state that true worship consists of worship in spirit **OR** worship in truth. Jesus clearly stated repeatedly that true worship is in spirit **AND** in truth. If either of these conditions are not met, then the equation does not equal true worship. These two are constants that have to co-exist in order for the result to be true worship. In other words, whilst we have seen and would agree that:

$$\text{Worship In Flesh} + \text{Worship In Error} \neq \text{True Worship}$$
$$(\text{Wrong Focus}) \qquad (\text{Wrong Way})$$

In understanding that both conditions have to co-exist for there to be true worship, what we also now see is that:

$$\text{Worship In Spirit} + \text{Worship In Error} \neq \text{True Worship}$$
$$(\text{Right focus}) \qquad (\text{Wrong Way})$$

$$\text{AND}$$

$$\text{Worship In Flesh} + \text{Worship In Truth} \neq \text{True Worship}$$
$$(\text{Wrong Focus}) \qquad (\text{Right Way})$$

For worship to be considered true and the kind of worship that the Father is seeking it has to be done in both **SPIRIT** (right focus) **AND** in **TRUTH** (right way). It takes both of these elements working together for worship to be the kind that the Father is seeking. Any time that one of these conditions is not met, it means that the equation does not equal true worship. It doesn't matter if one of these conditions is true or right. Any time that one of these elements is missing the equation doesn't meet the standard of true! As this began to sink in, I was quite challenged by the Lord as I considered the implications that this presented to my own worship.

Such is not meant to come across as condemnatory, but rather to open our eyes to the fact that God has very clearly laid out for us the requirements of what true worship is. Whilst it is a simple equation, if very clearly details that both conditions have to be met in order for true worship to be the result. If we are not meeting both of these then we are not offering true worship.

What struck me as I considered this was that whilst it may be very easy to spot worship that doesn't meet both the conditions of true worship, i.e. when it is not done in spirit and not done in truth, it is not quite so simple to spot when only one condition is missing. It is very easy to assume and to justify that we are offering true worship when we are meeting one of these requirements. When one of these conditions is met, the worship itself has an air of authenticity, but the reality is that it still does not meet the standard of true! Our worship may be done with a complete focus on the Spirit and be Spirit led, but we may not be completely aligned to the truths of the Word. This type of worship is harder to identify as the worship itself seems genuinely authentic. Similarly, our worship may be done completely according to the truths of the Word, but it may lack the Spirit. Again, this type of worship more closely resembles true worship, but as it does not have both constants it still falls short. In order for our worship to be true worship it must be done in spirit and in truth.

> *God is Spirit, and those **who worship Him must** worship in spirit and truth." (Joh 4:24) NKJV*

What also struck me is that there are more equations that result in worship not being true than there are ones that result in true worship. There is but one standard for true and one standard alone. Such is the truth of scripture. Whilst man may try to justify various ways of doing things, God is very clear time and time again that He has standards that man is to meet.

> *"Enter by the narrow gate; for wide is the gate and broad is the way that leads to destruction, and there are many who go in by it. Because narrow is the gate and difficult is the way which leads to life, and there are few who find it. (Mat 7:13-14) NKJV*

We may have the mindset that worship is a straightforward matter, and this is no doubt a similar mindset to what the Samaritan woman had! What we can see from these verses of John though is that the Lord has a very clear definition of what true worship is to Him. It is not something that He has left to man to define, He has succinctly laid out what the qualifications of true worship are. Whilst the equation is not complicated; it is one that takes personal reflection and careful consideration of what God considers to be true compared to what we think it is and subsequently offer from our understanding.

Summary

As I considered 'The Standard of True' we have discovered in this section, I was stirred by the fact that this is the type of worshipper that the Father is seeking. The Father is seeking His people to worship Him in this way. In fact, the words of Jesus were that we **must** worship in this way. There was no option given here by Jesus, but rather a directive. This is how we must worship. As believers the Lord has called us to worship in this way. He is looking for this kind of worship from His people and His Church.

The question then becomes; how do we fulfill this? How do we be the true worshippers that the Father is looking for? How do we make sure we meet the standard of true? To answer this, we need to take a deeper look at each of the conditions mentioned above. That is, we need to gain an understanding of what it is to worship in the spirit versus worship in the flesh. Likewise, we need to look at what it means to worship in error versus what it means to worship in truth. It is only in gaining a greater biblical understanding of these facets that we can then examine our own worship and make sure that it meets the standards that the Lord has set. To understand these is to understand the differences that exist and through deepening our understanding we can be safeguarded from ever straying from the conditions required of true worship.

It is my belief that the Church over the past few years has been in a season of refining. The Lord has been calling His people back to the truths of His Word, and in this current season He is wanting to deepen our understanding surrounding worship. Across the world, the Lord is focusing in on this theme. The Lord is seeking and calling His people to rise as true worshippers.

It is my prayer that as you read through this text you will likewise be stirred by the Lord to be a worshipper that meets the standard of true.

In Flesh Or In Spirit

In Flesh Or In Spirit

In this section we will consider the first part of the standard of true worship, what it means to worship in spirit as opposed to what it means to worship in flesh. The danger that exists for us is that although we may be worshipping the Lord, if we are doing it in the flesh rather than in spirit, then we are falling short of the standard of true worship. The call of Jesus in John was that as believers we are called to be those who worship in spirit and not in the flesh.

Throughout the Word of God, the flesh and the Spirit are constantly described as being in opposition to one another. Time and again the writers of scripture highlight the positives of the Spirit compared to the negatives of the flesh:

> *That which is born of the **flesh** is **flesh**; and that which is born of the **Spirit** is **spirit**. (Joh 3:6) KJV*

> *For he who sows to his **flesh** will of the **flesh** reap corruption, but he who sows to the **Spirit** will of the **Spirit** reap everlasting life. (Gal 6:8) NKJV*

> *That the righteous requirement of the law might be fulfilled in us who do not walk according to the **flesh** but according to the **Spirit**. For those who live according to the **flesh** set their minds on the things of the **flesh**, but those who live according to the **Spirit**, the things of the **Spirit**. For to be carnally minded is death, but to be spiritually minded is life and peace. Because the carnal mind is enmity against God; for it is not subject to the law*

> *of God, nor indeed can be. So then, those who are in the **flesh** cannot please God. But you are not in the **flesh** but in the **Spirit**, if indeed the **Spirit** of God dwells in you. Now if anyone does not have the Spirit of Christ, he is not His. (Rom 8:4-9) NKJV*

> *It is the **Spirit** who gives life; the **flesh** profits nothing. The words that I speak to you are spirit, and they are life. (Joh 6:63) NKJV*

> *Are you so foolish? Having begun in the **Spirit**, are you now being made perfect by the **flesh**? (Gal 3:3) NKJV*

> *Watch and pray, lest you enter into temptation. The **spirit** indeed is willing, but the **flesh** is weak." (Mar 14:38) NKJV*

> *But as then he that was born after the **flesh** persecuted him that was born after the **Spirit**, even so it is now. Nevertheless what saith the scripture? Cast out the bondwoman and her son: for the son of the bondwoman shall not be heir with the son of the freewoman. So then, brethren, we are not children of the bondwoman, but of the free. (Gal 4:29-31) KJV*

Throughout the Word of God, and the New Testament in particular, the writers constantly use the flesh and the Spirit in a contrastive sense. The Spirit and the flesh are both realities that exist in the life of every believer. We though are called to be of the Spirit and to put away the things of the flesh. There is to be a separation and a prioritisation that needs to happen in the lives of those who follow Christ.

This is not always straight forward though. As has been stated earlier in the study and shown by the above verses, the flesh and the Spirit war against each other in and throughout the life of every believer. Whilst we will seek to grow in the Spirit and let go of the flesh, the flesh will always try to reestablish its grip in our lives and suffocate the Spirit. Whilst the Spirit tries to lift us up, the flesh tries to pull us down. As Paul states in Galatians 5:

> *For the **flesh** lusts against the **Spirit**, and the **Spirit** against the **flesh**; and **these are contrary to one another**, so that you do not do the things that you wish. (Gal 5:17) NKJV*

The thought behind the Greek word for 'contrary' as used here means those things that are opposites, they withstand each other, they are contrary and can't co-exist. The more we are filled with one, the less we are filled with the other. It is a principle that works both ways! More Spirit equals less flesh, but more flesh equals less Spirit.

In focusing in on the topic of worship that we are called to offer unto the Lord, we again see these two elements in opposition. The flesh and the Spirit pull against each other in our worship of the Lord. As has been said, there is a tug war that goes on between these two forces seeking the focus of the individual in worship. Worship in Spirit involves having a right focus, it is a focus solely on the Spirit. Worshipping in the Flesh on the other hand involves having a wrong focus, a focus on the flesh. In worship the battle between the Spirit and the flesh centres on where our focus is. Whether our focus in worship is on the Spirit or whether our focus in worship is on the flesh determines whether our worship is true worship.

But what exactly does that look like, and how does scripture reveal this? What does worship in the flesh look like and how is worship in the Spirit different? These are questions that we will seek to answer as we move forward. In this section we will consider worship in flesh and worship in Spirit separately initially to see what they individually look like from a biblical perspective. As we do this, we will elaborate on the thoughts provided here and those discussed earlier before expounding on how we can identify where our focus in worship is and how we can correct it if necessary. We will then finish the section by considering some warning signs that can indicate if our focus in worship may need a readjustment.

As believers we need a Godly discernment to reflect on our worship and see if we are reaching the standard of true. For us to meet the standard of true, our focus needs to be on the Spirit and on the Spirit alone.

Worship in Flesh

*For those **who live according to the flesh set their minds on the things of the flesh**, but those who live according to the Spirit, the things of the Spirit. (Rom 8:5)*
NKJV

In this section we will spend some time considering what worship in the flesh is, what it looks like and how we can identify it. It should be noted that in doing this, the intention is not to provide tools for us to judge the worship of others, but rather to provide insights for us to be able to consider our own worship and if we are meeting the standard of true. The points that are provided are ones that should provoke introspection in each of our lives.

In the above verse Paul stated that those "that are after the flesh do mind the things of the flesh". That may seem fairly obvious, but what does that actually look like? We could actually rephrase Paul's statement to read "those who are after the flesh are focused on those things which satisfy and please self". Any time that flesh has the focus there is a focus on self: self-satisfaction, self-interest, self-promotion, self-glorification, self-seeking etc, etc. The flesh is focused on itself and what it gets out of any situation, opportunity, event or relationship. The flesh switches the focus from the external to the internal and 'I' becomes the focal point. 'I' this and 'I' that; 'this pleases me', 'that doesn't please me'; 'I' like that, 'I' want that. It is 'I' and self that dictate the focus. The flesh is only ever concerned about itself and how to satisfy itself.

This same truth is seen with worship in flesh. Worship in flesh is only concerned about itself in worship. When worship is done in the flesh the focus is on self or on 'I'. The act of worship itself may appear genuine, and whilst it may not be immediately obvious, when flesh is involved in worship the focus on self is always there. When worship is done in flesh the focus is on the worshipper rather than the one whom should be worshipped.

Let us consider some scriptural examples that highlight this focus of self or 'I' in relation to worship in flesh.

The Introduction of Self

It is important that we understand that in the beginning self had no part in worship. In the beginning worship was perfect and was undertaken in Spirit alone. In the beginning worship always met the standard of true, it was pure worship and never deviated from this. There was a period of time where self and worship were never linked. But there came a point where self was introduced and subsequently infected worship and that which was once perfect became corrupted.

This introduction of self and worship happened with Lucifer, otherwise known as Satan. In scripture Lucifer is referred to at various points, but there are two passages of scripture that give us great insight into Lucifer and particularly into his fall. These are Ezekiel 28:1-19 and Isaiah 14:4-23. Both of these are prophetical words, and both passages involve a term known as the law of double reference. The law of double reference ascertains that the language of a passage indicates that whilst the words of the passage may be directed to an individual they are also speaking to another person or being beyond or behind that person. It is the language of the passage that makes this clear.

A great example of this is seen when Jesus rebukes Peter as recorded in Matt 16. There we read that Jesus had asked the disciples who man said He was. Having received the response of who others thought He was, Jesus then challenged His disciples as to who they thought He was. Peter replied that Jesus was the Christ, the son of the living God. It was a clear profession of faith by Peter in who Jesus was. Jesus then blessed Peter and told him that he would receive the keys of the kingdom and that whatever he bound on earth will be bound in heaven and whatever he loosed on earth would be loosed in heaven. It was quite a blessing.

Following this, Jesus then went onto explain to His disciples how He would soon go to Jerusalem where He would suffer many things, be killed but then be raised again the third day. In response to Jesus words, Peter rebuked Jesus for this declaring 'this shall not be'. Jesus then turned to Peter and said:

> *But He turned and said to Peter,* **"Get behind Me, Satan!** *You are an offense to Me, for you are not mindful of the things of God, but the things of men." (Mat 16:23) NKJV*

When we read this verse, we know that despite the plain reading of scripture, Jesus was not calling Peter Satan. He was not associating the two. What we see here is a clear example of the law of double reference. In speaking to Peter Jesus was actually addressing the spirit behind the thought of Peter. In speaking to Peter, Jesus was actually talking to the individual who planted this thought and motivated this utterance from Peter.

With this understanding of the law of double reference, we will look at Ezekiel 28:1-19 to see what it reveals to us about Lucifer. For our purposes here we will just consider a few verses, but I would encourage you to read over the entire passage from Ezekial 28.

> *"Son of man, take up a lamentation for the king of Tyre, and say to him, 'Thus says the Lord GOD: "You were the seal of perfection, Full of wisdom and perfect in beauty. You were in Eden, the garden of God; Every precious stone was your covering: The sardius, topaz, and diamond, Beryl, onyx, and jasper, Sapphire, turquoise, and emerald with gold. The workmanship of your timbrels and pipes Was prepared for you on the day you were created. "You were the anointed cherub who covers; I established you; You were on the holy mountain of God; You walked back and forth in the midst of fiery stones.* **You were**

> ***perfect** in your ways from the day you were created, **Till iniquity was found in you**. (Eze 28:12-15) NKJV*

As we read this passage it should be clear that Ezekiel was not addressing the king of Tyre in these verses. The language is simply not applicable to him. The king of Tyre was not in Eden and he was not the anointed Cherub. The language here is directed to Lucifer, i.e. Satan. He is the king behind the kingdoms of the world. Just as lucifer was behind the thoughts of Peter, so to was he behind the rule of the king of Tyrus.

From this passage there a several things that we can glean in regard to Lucifer.

1) Lucifer was the seal of perfection.
2) Lucifer was full of wisdom and perfect in beauty.
3) Lucifer walked in Eden.
4) Lucifer was covered in precious stones. Interesting to note that this is a very similar covering to that which sat upon Aaron as High Priest. (v13 with Ex 28:15-21)
5) Lucifer is a created being, and he was created perfectly.
6) Lucifer had tabrets and pipes. These are musical instruments.
7) These instruments were prepared by God for Lucifer in the day of his creation. Lucifer was a being created with worship in mind.
8) Lucifer was the anointed cherub who covers.
9) The Lord set and established Lucifer as the anointed cherub.
10) Lucifer had been upon the holy mountain of God.
11) Lucifer had walked up and down in the midst of the stones of fire.
12) Lucifer was perfect from the day of his creation.
13) There came a day though when iniquity was found in Lucifer. (v15)

Lucifers name itself means day star, son of the morning or light bearer. He is held by expositors to be an arch angel, one of three explicitly mentioned in scripture. Michael in scripture is the arch angel associated with Jesus, Garbiel is the arch angel seen linked with the Holy Spirit and Lucifer is linked in scripture as the arch angel associated with the Father. This is the thought we see in verse 14 of Ezekial in describing Lucifer as the anointed Cherub the covers.

Lucifer is generally held by expositors as the archangel in charge of the worship of Heaven. He was the worship leader, created by God and having instruments created for him to fulfill this role. It was an office he was perfect in from the day he was created until iniquity was found in him. There came a point where Lucifer fell. Whilst Ezekiel tells us that iniquity was found in Lucifer, he doesn't tell us what this iniquity was or give us any details about this.

1 Timothy 3:6 tells us that it was pride that led to Lucifers fall, but it is in Isaiah 14 that we glean our greatest understanding of what Lucifers iniquity was. In Isaiah 14 we read of the prophet Isaiah being commanded of the Lord to speak to the king of Babylon. Several verses into this passage, the prophet switches mid prophecy and starts speaking in regard to Lucifer, the principality behind the king. The passage is quoted in full here and I would encourage to take the time to read and then reread it and consider what it reveals about Lucifers iniquity.

> *"How you are fallen from heaven, O Lucifer, son of the morning! How you are cut down to the ground, You who weakened the nations! For you have said in your heart: 'I will ascend into heaven, I will exalt my throne above the stars of God; I will also sit on the mount of the congregation On the farthest sides of the north; I will ascend above the heights of the clouds, I will be like the Most High.' Yet you shall be brought down to Sheol, To the lowest depths of the Pit. (Isa 14:12-15) NKJV*

Notice how many times 'I' is used in this passage! There are five specific 'I' statements uttered by Lucifer. In this passage Lucifer is recorded as having stated:

1) **I WILL** ascend into heaven.
   Self-will. This wasn't Gods will, this was what Lucifer wanted.

2) **I WILL** exalt my throne.
   Self-exaltation. What throne? Lucifer didn't have a throne! He was the arch angel who covered the Lord's throne, but here we see his desire for his own throne.

3) **I WILL** sit upon the mount of the congregation.
   Self-enthronement. Not just a throne, but one that he would enthrone himself upon above the congregation.

4) **I WILL** ascend above the heights.
   Self-ascension.

5) **I WILL** be like the most High.
   Self-deification. A desire not to just be like God but to be God.

The whole focus of Lucifer was on self. Self-will, self-exaltation, self-enthronement, self-deification, self-promotion, self-seeking, self-glorification. It is a clear and total focus on self that puffed Lucifer up in pride. It was a focus that brought about Lucifers fall. What we see here is the iniquity talked about by Ezekiel. Ezekiel gives us insight into the office of Lucifer whereas Isaiah gives us insight into the fall of Lucifer. With Lucifer there came a point in time where iniquity was found in him because his focus shifted. Lucifer fell from his office because his focus in worship shifted from Spirit to self.

In this example we see a twist in worship. There was a shift in focus that occurred. Prior to this all worship had been holy, pure and had met the divine standard. Here though we see the introduction of self into worship. This was the start of worship falling short of Gods standard of true. Lucifers attention turned from what he could give in worship to what he could receive. His outward focus shifted to an inward one and with it, self became exalted. Lucifer took the worship that was intended for God and instead made it all about himself. It all became about 'I'. 'I will, I will, I will, I will, I will'.

This is the first instance of flesh or self in worship, but it is the seed from which all of our proceeding examples flow. Any form of self in worship traces its roots back to here. Self seeks to take the glory away from the Lord in worship and give it to itself. When we understand this root of self in worship, it should cause us to have a realisation of the seriousness of any form of self in our worship. When we understand where it started, then we begin to understand that no part of self in worship can ever glorify God or meet His standard of true.

Cain and Abel

The next example of self in worship that we will consider in that of Cain and Abel. This account is recorded for us in Genesis 4:

> *Then she bore again, this time his brother Abel. Now Abel was a keeper of sheep, but Cain was a tiller of the ground. And in the process of time it came to pass that Cain brought an offering of the fruit of the ground to the LORD. Abel also brought of the firstborn of his flock and of their fat. And the LORD respected Abel and his offering, but He did not respect Cain and his offering. And Cain was very angry, and his countenance fell. So the LORD said to Cain, "Why are you angry? And why has your countenance fallen? If you do well, will you not be accepted? And if you do not do well, sin lies at the door. And its desire is for you, but you should rule over it." Now Cain talked with Abel his brother; and it came to pass, when they were in the field, that Cain rose up against Abel his brother and killed him. Then the LORD said to Cain, "Where is Abel your brother?" He said, "I do not know. Am I my brother's keeper?" And He said, "What have you done? The voice of your brother's blood cries out to Me from the ground. So now you are cursed from the*

> *earth, which has opened its mouth to receive your brother's blood from your hand. (Gen 4:2-11) NKJV*

In this passage we read that sometime after the fall of Adam and Eve, both Cain and Abel brought and presented offerings unto the Lord. Cain we are told brought of the fruit of the ground, whereas Abel brought from the firstlings of the flock. As these were presented unto the Lord God looked with respect on Abel's offering, but He did not look favourably on Cain's. This caused jealousy and anger to rise in Cain and despite a warning from the Lord about where those feelings would lead, Cain's anger festered, and he arose against his brother in a jealousy fuelled rage and killed him.

As we consider this narrative of Cain and Abel we can see that the central piece of it is the worship of God. It was unto God that both men were bringing their offerings. Both men were coming before the Lord in a worshipful act, and it was because of the worship that Abel offered, and the Lord's response to it, that he would subsequently be killed by his brother. With approaching God in worship being at the core of this account for both men, we may well ask what prompted such a contrary response in Cain? How did he go from worship to murder?

To answer this, there are a few things that we must first consider from the Genesis account.

GOD HAD ALREADY REVEALED THE STANDARD FOR WORSHIP.

In Genesis 3 we read of the fall of man when Adam and Eve ate of the forbidden fruit. When Adam and Eve partook, we are told that their eyes were opened, and they realised that they were both naked. To hide their nakedness, they sowed fig leaves together and made coverings for themselves. Later though the Lord came to the garden and after Adam and Eve had admitted their transgression, the Lord then pronounced a sentence upon them and the serpent. Following this though, the Lord did one final thing for Adam and Eve. Genesis 3:21 tells us:

> *Unto Adam also and to his wife **did the LORD God make coats of skins**, and clothed them. (Gen 3:21) KJV*

The question we need to consider here is why did the Lord make Adam and Eve coats of skins? Adam and Eve had already covered their nakedness with the fig leaves they had sown together! The fig leaves though were a man made covering and the truth revealed through God's actions here is that man's efforts could never cover the consequences of sin. God here took away that which man had created to cover his sin and instead gave unto him coats of skin, a Godly covering that had come from the death of a substitute victim. An animal was killed for the coats to be given, but the animal wasn't killed for the sole purpose of providing clothing. The animals were killed because as the book of Hebrews tells us the only thing that can take away the stain of sin is blood.

> *And according to the law almost all things are purified with blood, **and without shedding of blood there is no remission**. (Heb 9:22) NKJV*

The coats of skin that came from the Lord revealed to Adam and Eve His sacrificial system of atonement. The only means of atonement for sin is that of the death of a substitute victim and the provision of innocent blood. In this instance God himself set forth for Adam and Eve the sacrifice and having atoned for their sins, He clothed them with coats of redemption. God cleansed, He covered, and He demonstrated unto Adam and Eve how He was to be approached in worship. It was here that God set forth His standard for sacrificial worship.

THE GROUND HAD BEEN CURSED.

Genesis 4 tells us that Cain was a tiller of the ground and that it was from what he produced that Cain brough forth fruit as an offering unto the Lord.

> *Then she bore again, this time his brother Abel. Now Abel was a keeper of sheep, **but Cain was a tiller of the ground**. And in the process of time it came to pass that **Cain brought***

> ***an offering of the fruit of the ground*** *to the LORD.*
> *(Gen 4:2-3) NKJV*

A chapter earlier though, in Genesis 3, we read that as part of the judgement upon Adam and Eve for their sin, God cursed the ground:

> *Then to Adam He said, "Because you have heeded the voice of your wife, and have eaten from the tree of which I commanded you, saying, 'You shall not eat of it':* ***"Cursed is the ground for your sake; In toil you shall eat of it All the days of your life.*** *Both thorns and thistles it shall bring forth for you, And you shall eat the herb of the field.* ***In the sweat of your face you shall eat bread*** *Till you return to the ground, For out of it you were taken; For dust you are, And to dust you shall return." (Gen 3:17-19) NKJV*

When Adam and Eve sinned, God cursed the ground. It would not only produce good plants, but it would now also produce thorns and thistles. Further to this, rather than the ground readily bringing forth its fruit for man to eat, it would require effort and sweat on the part of man to produce a crop. In other words, growing fruit and vegetables was going to be hard work.

At the start of Genesis 4 Cain is described for us as "a tiller of the ground". The word tiller in the Hebrew means "to *work* (in any sense); by implication to *serve*, *till*, (causatively) *enslave*, etc". This word carries with it the sense of bondage and enslavement. Cain, as a tiller, served the ground, he was enslaved to it. Cain would have worked hard to produce that which he brought unto the Lord. He had to work the ground and protect his crops from thorns and weeds. This was all done through the sweat, toil and effort of Cain. Cain had to serve the ground to get the produce that he wanted, and it was from these **works** that he brough an offering unto the Lord.

MAN WAS NOT YET ALLOWED TO EAT MEAT.

Whilst Cain was a tiller of the ground, Abel was a keeper of the sheep. In a natural way of thinking this makes sense as one brother was looking after the vegetables, whilst the other was looking after the meat. But this wasn't the case. At this point in time man was not yet eating meat!

In Genesis 1 we read that the Lord gave man every herb and every fruit tree as his source of food:

> *And God said,* **"See, I have given you every herb that yields seed which is on the face of all the earth, and every tree whose fruit yields seed; to you it shall be for food.** *Also, to every beast of the earth, to every bird of the air, and to everything that creeps on the earth, in which there is life, I have given every green herb for food"; and it was so. (Gen 1:29-30) NKJV*

The herbs of the ground and the fruit of the trees were to be the meat of man. In Genesis 1, God had just created all of the animals, but He did not give them unto man to eat, He only gave unto man the herbs and the fruit as food. In the beginning the food of man was completely plant based!

In fact, it was not until the time of Noah, after the flood had come upon the earth, that man was given permission to eat meat.

> *So God blessed Noah and his sons, and said to them: "Be fruitful and multiply, and fill the earth. And the fear of you and the dread of you shall be on every beast of the earth, on every bird of the air, on all that move on the earth, and on all the fish of the sea. They are given into your hand.* **Every moving thing that lives shall be food for you.** *I have given you all things, even as the green herbs. But you shall not eat flesh with its life, that is, its blood. (Gen 9:1-4) NKJV*

The Hebrew word for food in this passage is the exact same word that is used for food in Genesis 1. This word is translated as "consume, devour, eat, food, meat". It is referring to that which the Lord permitted man to partake of.

From Genesis 1 through to Genesis 9, man was an herbivore not an omnivore. Man did not start eating meat until after the flood. With that being the case, we may then ask why was Abel a keeper of the flock? Why was Abel a shepherd if man was not allowed to eat meat? Why such care for something that did not have a benefit to man? Was it because they were following the example of clothing that the Lord had given them in Genesis 3? Possibly, but how large a flock would you need for the limited population of that time? How many clothes would they go through to warrant someone having the designated task of being a keeper of the flocks?

In contemplating this I would put forth something else for you to consider. Could it be possible that Abel in being a keeper of the flocks was actually ensuring that there was always sufficient means to worship the Lord? God had shown to man how He must be worshipped back in Genesis 3, and for that to happen according to Gods way there had to be a ready supply of sacrifices. Abel in keeping the flock, was ensuring that man could always approach God in worship according to the Lord's standard. Abel was a man of faith, and one who worshipped in Spirit (Heb 11:4). He understood the Lord's way of approach and never wanted to stray from that. His whole life centred around worship.

From these points we see that Cain would have known the way to worship the Lord. His parents would have told him and no doubt he would have grown up seeing them worship the Lord. He would have been well versed in the correct way to approach God in worship just as his brother Abel had been. Cain though was a blood of the lamb rejector. Even though Cain was well aware of how to approach the Lord, he rejected the route of sacrifice. He instead chose to bring to the Lord something that he worked for. Cain was a tiller of the ground, and he brought unto the Lord that which he had sweated over. Rather than approach in faith, Cain approached with self-works. It was worship rooted in self. Cain's approach was that I am bringing unto you something that I have worked for and something that I think you should be blessed with. You should be blessed by the effort that it has taken me to produce this. Look how good what I am bringing is. How much better, nicer, lovelier is what I have presented compared to the mess of my brother. This required my strength, my time, my persistence and I feel you should be blessed by it. The approach of Cain was one completely rooted in self. The whole focus was on Cain and Cain's efforts. Look at me!

Cain was essentially saying to the Lord this is how I will worship you. I am setting aside the way you have directed because the way that I have chosen makes me feel good and this makes me feel like I have sacrificed. I feel good worshipping you in this way. It brings me satisfaction.

The result of course was that the Lord didn't look on Cain's offering with favour. He wasn't pleased with it, and He didn't accept it. How could He? How could God ever be pleased with worship that was more focused on self than on Him?

In response to this, rather than being humbled, anger arose in Cain. His whole attitude was essentially why aren't you blessed or pleased with what I want to give to you? You accepted Abel's worship, but mine is much better, more pleasing to look at, has cost more. It took a lot of effort for me to grow these. I worked hard. This focus on self continues to grow as the narrative continues. The resulting actions of Cain in slaying his brother and in his discourse with the Lord further highlight this focus of Cain. The flesh always reacts when its needs aren't met! If Cain had truly been trying to worship in spirit, then we would have at some point seen genuine repentance from him. Perhaps when his initial offering was not accepted, or when the Lord warned him about his attitudes or after he had slain his brother. But we don't! We never see an attitude of repentance!

Any true worshipper who saw their offering not be accepted by the Lord, would be humbled and convicted in heart to seek and repent before the Lord in order find out why they had fallen short. A true worshipper wouldn't turn the other way when their worship wasn't accepted, they would press in and seek the Lord in order to grow and offer true worship unto Him. It would actually cause a true worshipper to seek the Lord, not push Him away as we see with Cain. Cain's worship was focused completely on self and when self didn't get the recognition it wanted or thought it deserved, it acted out, lashed out and struck out. Cain's worship was entirely focused on the flesh and from this seed we see the works of the flesh evident through Cain's actions; hatred, wrath, strife, envying's, murder etc (Gal 5:19-21).

Cain's approach highlights to us the desire of self to be satisfied through the worship that we give. Self wants to approach the Lord in its way and feel good about it, and self wants its efforts to be recognised. Externally it may have a right appearance, but the truth of the matter is that it is wanting self-recognition for its act. Any worship based in works, that makes us feel like we have sacrificed or is based in how we want to worship the Lord has elements of self within it. It is a wrong focus and is one that we as believers should not have. We need to worship as Abel and not Cain.

Eli's Sons

The next example for us to consider is with the sons of Eli the Priest that we read about in 1 Samuel 2. Whilst Eli was a good man, his sons where evil and are described in scripture as being sons of Belial, who knew not the Lord. These are extremely harsh words, but even more so when we consider that this is referring to individuals who were in the office of priests unto the Lord.

Eli's sons were wicked men who had no regard for their father and did as they pleased (1 Sam 2:25). They did not care who their actions affected or hurt; they were only focused on themselves. With Eli's sons we see individuals who were totally focused on self-fulfilment, self-pleasure and self-will.

In terms of how we see the evidence of self in their worship, in 1 Sam 2:12-16 we read:

> *Now the sons of Eli were corrupt; they did not know the LORD. And* **the priests' custom** *with the people was that when any man offered a sacrifice, the priest's servant would come with a three-pronged fleshhook in his hand while the meat was boiling. Then he would thrust it into the pan, or kettle, or caldron, or pot; and the priest would take for himself all that the fleshhook brought up. So they did in Shiloh to all the Israelites who came there. Also, before they burned the fat, the priest's servant would come and say to the man who sacrificed, "Give*

meat for roasting to the priest, for he will not take boiled meat from you, but raw." And if the man said to him, "They should really burn the fat first; then you may take as much as your heart desires," he would then answer him, "No, but you must give it now; and if not, I will take it by force." (1Sa 2:12-16) NKJV

This passage describes the interactions that Eli's sons had with the people of Israel when they came to bring their sacrifices unto the Lord in Worship. There are two major issues raised here relating to the worship of the people.

THE PRIESTS PORTION.

In Leviticus and Exodus, we are very clearly told by the Lord what the priests portion was to be and what should happen with the fat of the offerings. Leviticus 7 tells us that:

> **And the priest shall burn the fat on the altar, but the breast shall be Aaron's and his sons'. Also the right thigh you shall give to the priest as a heave offering from the sacrifices of your peace offerings.** *He among the sons of Aaron, who offers the blood of the peace offering and the fat, shall have the right thigh for his part. For the breast of the wave offering and the thigh of the heave offering I have taken from the children of Israel, from the sacrifices of their peace offerings, and I have given them to Aaron the priest and to his sons from the children of Israel by a statute forever.' " This is the consecrated portion for Aaron and his sons, from the offerings made by fire to the LORD, on the day when Moses presented them to minister to the LORD as priests. The LORD commanded this to be given to them by the children of Israel, on the day that He anointed them, by a statute forever throughout their generations. (Lev 7:31-36) NKJV*

See also Exo 29:27.

The Lord very clearly laid out what was the portion for the priests. The priests were assigned the meat of the breast and the shoulder. What we see in 1 Samuel is that the sons of Eli were not satisfied with their portion and chose to take more than they were allocated. They would take a flesh hook and take extra from that which was being boiled according to "the priests custom", but not the Lord's!

Eli's sons were unsatisfied with what they received from the worship of the Lord, and they elected to be disobedient to the Levitical laws and seize, by force if necessary, that which they wanted to receive out of worship. They were taking more than what their portion was from the worship of the Lord. In doing this they were actually taking from what was the Lord's portion in order to satisfy themselves. They were robbing God to satisfy their flesh.

THE FAT WAS TO BE BURNT.

The Lord had also very explicitly laid out what was to happen with the fat of the offerings. The fat of the offering was to be burnt upon the altar. The Lord was actually even more detailed about the fat of offerings and just a few verses prior to the above quoted passage we read:

> *For whoever eats the fat of the animal of which men offer an offering made by fire to the LORD, the person who eats it shall be cut off from his people. (Lev 7:25)* NKJV

It was because of this law that the people wanted to let the fat be burnt. They knew what was required of their worship. The sons of Eli though disregarded the people and the Lord and demanded a greater portion, and if it wasn't bad enough that they were taking more than they should, they also did this before the fat was burnt according to the law.

While the priests demanded these things, they didn't do this themselves, they sent their servants to do this task and in so doing the sons of Eli's corrupted others. The priests' servants would demand the portion before an individual had even burnt the fat of their offering unto the Lord. If an individual resisted them then it would be taken by force. What a heinous picture this paints, people threatened with violence whilst trying to worship their Lord. The sons of Eli were willing for the worship of the people to be hindered so that their flesh would be satisfied. Their focus was on self.

Having seen that there were ordinances of the Lord, and that the priests had clearly laid out guidelines about what to do with the fat and what portion of the sacrifices was theirs, why did the sons of Eli act like this? Why would they act so contrary to the law?

Whilst the people had a focus of coming before the Lord and worshipping Him, that was not the focus of Eli's sons. They had no regard for the worship of the people and absolutely no regard for worship according to God's standards. They completely disregarded that which the Lord had stipulated surrounding worship. The only focus that Eli's sons had in regard to worship was themselves and what they got out of worship. Their focus was on what worship did for them.

The offerings of the people were first and foremost the Lords before then becoming the provision of the priests. But that was not how Eli's sons viewed worship. Their view was this is what I want to get out of worship. "I don't want that, I want this". "I want to satisfy the desires of my flesh". "I want to satisfy self". "Worship is about satisfying my needs".

Whilst this is a terrible attitude for any of us to have in worship, it is even more so in this case when we consider that Eli's sons were functioning in the role of priests. As priests their focus in worship was not on God, but only on themselves and their needs and wants in worship. Their focus was on what made them feel good in worship. Can you imagine the flow on affects this would have had on the people who were seeking to genuinely worship the Lord and instead were met with threats of violence and were being inhibited from offering their worship by the priests of the Lord? It would certainly not have encouraged the People in their worship of the Lord!

The focus of Eli's sons in worship was on how worship satisfied self. It is another aspect of self in worship, self-satisfaction. They didn't care about how their actions affected the worship of the Lord or the individuals offering the worship. They were only focused on what worship did for them.

The Pharisee and the Publican

In Luke 18 we are given the parable of the pharisee and the publican by Jesus. There we read:

> *Also He spoke this parable to some who trusted in themselves that they were righteous, and despised others: "Two men went up to the temple to pray, one a Pharisee and the other a tax collector. The Pharisee stood and prayed thus with himself, 'God, I thank You that I am not like other men—extortioners, unjust, adulterers, or even as this tax collector. I fast twice a week; I give tithes of all that I possess.' And the tax collector, standing afar off, would not so much as raise his eyes to heaven, but beat his breast, saying, 'God, be merciful to me a sinner!' I tell you, this man went down to his house justified rather than the other; for everyone who exalts himself will be humbled, and he who humbles himself will be exalted." (Luk 18:9-14) NKJV*

In this passage we read of two individuals who were coming before the Lord in worship. Both of these men were going up to the temple to pray. The Pharisee approached God with confidence and declared all of the amazing acts he had done and how that in comparison to other men he was pretty good. The publican though stood afar off; he would not come close unto the Lord. He was aware of his own shortcomings and in humility sought the forgiveness of the Lord.

This account actually has a lot of similarities to that of Cain and Abel. We see that here that one approach was by works and the other approach was by faith! Note the statement of the pharisee again this time specifically focusing in on his focus on works and self:

> *The Pharisee stood and prayed thus with himself, 'God, **I thank You that I am not like other men**—extortioners, unjust, adulterers, or even as this tax collector. **I fast twice** a week; **I give tithes** of all that **I possess**.' (Luk 18:11-12) NKJV*

The Pharisee based his approach unto the Lord on the fact that his works qualified him to do so. As we read over his statement there is such an obvious focus on self. His worship was wrapped around I. 'I' thank thee, that 'I' am this good and 'I' do all of these things. I'm so amazing. It is just I, I, I. His approach to the Lord is completely self-focused. It is an approach of pride with a focus on self. (Note also the five uses of 'I')

The Publican on the other hand approached in complete humility. He didn't mention I, he didn't mention self. All he spoke of was his complete and utter need for the mercy of the Father. The approach of the Publican mirrors that which we read of in the Psalms:

> *The sacrifices of God are a broken spirit, A broken and a contrite heart—These, O God, You will not despise. (Psa 51:17)* NKJV

The Publican brought an acceptable sacrifice. He approached the Lord with a focus on the spirit and not a focus on self. The publican didn't seek to exalt himself he sought to exalt God. The pharisee though sought to use worship as a means to exalt himself. It was a means for him to show off his religious piety. Worship was a vessel for the Pharisee to exalt himself and promote how great he was and how religiously superior he was. It was an approach in self.

Summary

And so, from the four examples that we have considered we have discovered from a Biblical perspective what worship that is in flesh looks like. Through each of these examples we have seen that the flesh is always looking for its own satisfaction. The flesh is always focused completely on self.

In the example of Lucifer, we saw how worship that was once perfect became defiled. Lucifer rose in pride, desiring for that which was given unto God to be given unto him. Lucifer looked for self-satisfaction in worship rather than having an attitude of self-sacrifice. Instead of dying to self, Lucifer engaged self. We see with Lucifer self-will, self-exaltation, self-enthronement, self-deification, self-promotion, self-seeking, self-glorification. Through Lucifer we see the introduction of self into worship.

We then saw how this seed that was birthed in Lucifer took hold in the hearts of men. Whilst Adam and Eve were shown and instructed by the Lord in how they were to worship, Cain let the seed of the flesh be sown in his heart. With Cain we saw how self wants to feel good about what it offers so it approaches in a way that it likes and that makes it feel good. It is about self-gratification in worship with no regards for the Lord's ways. The flow on from this is that it then subsequently wants its efforts in worship to be recognised. Self wants to be acknowledged and esteemed for its works in worship.

In 1 Samuel 2 we read of Eli's two sons, priests of the land, but were actually considered by the Lord as being sons of Belial. These two evil sons looked at how worship could benefit them and for what they could get out of it as they took the portions that they wanted from the offerings of the people against their will and contrary to the law of the Lord. These two highlight to us that worship in flesh is focused on what worship does for the giver. Its only concern is what it gets out of worship. There is little to no thought about giving in worship, only receiving.

Finally, with the Pharisee we see worship as a vessel to promote and exalt oneself. The Pharisee used worship as a stage from which he could broadcast himself to all that were in attendance. His worship was completely focused on self and self-promotion.

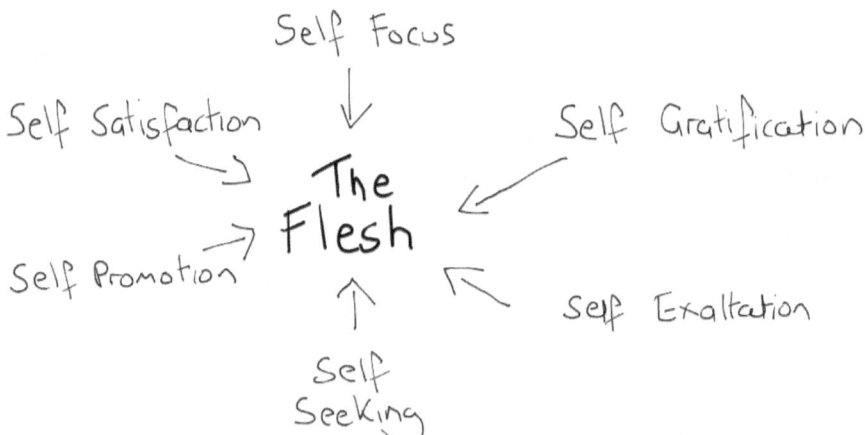

Through all of these example's time and again we see the truth that worship done in the flesh always looks to feed self in some way. It is self-interested worship, where the focus is less on God and more on the individual who is offering it. It is worship done for self-gratification.

This seed of self in worship that we have looked at with Cain, the sons of Eli and the Pharisee all trace their roots back to Lucifer. As has already been stated, when we see where worship in flesh with a focus on self originated, it should highlight to us the absolute necessity of having absolutely no part of flesh involved in the worship that we give. True worship can never have any focus on the flesh, for a focus on the flesh is a focus on self and if our focus is on self in worship then in reality, we are worshipping self and not God.

> *For those who live according to the flesh set their minds on the things of the flesh … (Rom 8:5) NKJV*

The flesh is always focused on itself. When we understand where the focus of the flesh is, we are more readily able to discern worship in flesh. We can identify the focus on self and the focus on 'I'.

Having looked at worship in flesh and its overwhelming focus on self, we have discovered some Biblical truths of how to identify if our worship is in the flesh. The question remains though, how do we identify worship in spirit and offer the true worship we are called to? This leads us to our next section.

Worship in Spirit

> *For those who live according to the flesh set their minds on the things of the flesh,* **but those who live according to the Spirit, the things of the Spirit.** *(Rom 8:5)* NKJV

Having seen what worship in the flesh looks like, we now turn our attention to considering worship in spirit. What does it mean to worship in spirit, what does that look like and how do we identify it? These are the questions that we will seek to answer in this section.

In reality the definition of worship in spirit is fairly straight forward. Whereas worship in flesh has a clear focus on self, with worship in spirit there is absolutely no focus on self. The flesh and the spirit are complete opposites. The flesh is focused on what pleases the flesh, but the spirit is focused on the things of the Spirit. Worship in spirit involves having absolutely no focus on self. The flesh and self have been completely removed and rather than being led by the flesh, we are led by the Spirit and keep in step with the focus of the Spirit.

> *If we* **live by the Spirit***, let us also keep* **in step with the Spirit.** *(Gal 5:25)* KJV

Whereas the flesh seeks to guide worship so that self is satisfied, when we worship in spirit, we are Spirit lead with a focus on giving in worship rather than receiving through it. Worship in spirit involves no focus on the flesh and no self-focus on 'I'. It is an outward focus based in humility rather than an inward one based on pride. It is a focus to give rather than receive.

It is a focus where the desires to satisfy the flesh and self have been removed.

In order to be able to worship in the spirit though, we have to have removed all elements of the flesh for we can only ever truly worship in Spirit when the flesh has been dealt with. For this to happen, there is a process that must happen in the life of every believer. It is a process of putting the flesh to death. Scripture refers to this as the process of **dying to self.** This is not a one and done event, but rather a process of discipline that believers must continually apply in their lives and in their walks with the Lord. It is only when we have dealt with the flesh that we can then truly worship in Spirit. To be focused on the Spirit, the flesh has to be removed. How do we do this though? Let's look at what scripture reveals to us.

Take up your cross

In Matthew 16:24-25 we read:

> *Then Jesus said to His disciples, "If anyone desires to come after Me, let him deny himself, and take up his cross, and follow Me. For whoever desires to save his life will lose it, but whoever loses his life for My sake will find it. (Mat 16:24-25) NKJV*

Having just explained to the disciples His own upcoming death and resurrection, Jesus then expanded on this thought and explained to His disciples what it truly meant to be a follower of Him. Within the passage Jesus was explaining to His disciples the concept of dying to self. Jesus was saying that for all who follow Him there is a dying to self that must occur.

If we focus in on Jesus words in verse 24, we see that within short verse there are four key points for us to take notice of in regard to dying to self:

IF ANY MAN WOULD COME AFTER ME.

What we see here is a choice. It is a choice that lays in the heart of each and every individual. To follow Jesus is a choice. It doesn't happen by accident or by chance, it happens when an individual determines that they are going to follow Christ.

Jesus gave context here to just who He was talking to and to whom the proceeding stipulations applied. "If you are going to follow me, then this is what is required". This is a call to those who would want to follow Jesus and to those that have already made that decision. This is a mandate to all who have accepted Him as their Saviour, and it is a call to every believer. It is an address to any who claim to be a follower of Jesus.

LET HIM DENY HIMSELF.

The first qualification for a follower of Jesus is a denial of self. For anyone who has accepted Christ as their saviour and chosen to follow Him, they **MUST** deny self. This is the starting point. To deny means to "deny utterly, to disown, to abstain". It involves recognising the appetites of the flesh and saying **'NO'**.

All of the focuses of self that we looked at in our previous section are to be abstained from and forgotten when we follow Jesus. Everything within us that looks for self-satisfaction and the promotion of self must be laid down. It involves starving the appetites of the flesh and not indulging them.

It is a process that requires a decision, honesty, discernment, accountability and ongoing commitment. To truly deny self involves not only having an understanding of how the flesh seeks to be fulfilled but also requires an open and honest introspection of ourselves. For this we need the guidance of the Spirit and a spirit of humility. Pride is a work of the flesh and will always resist the work of the Spirit. Humility though allows the Spirit to lead and guide us and the more we press in after the Spirit, the more He will reveal to us that which is within us that must be denied and laid down.

There is an onus that rests on us in this battle. The words of Jesus were let him deny himself. Having decided to follow Jesus **we** must then decide to deny the flesh. We can pray for strength in these moments, but ultimately it is still the individual who makes the choice, and it is a choice that has to be made on a daily basis. This is not a battle that will be won in a day, a week or a year. Whilst the appetites of the flesh may diminish the more that we deny them, we can never afford to rest on our laurels and presume the battle has been won. As believers we need to understand that, as scripture tells us, the flesh wars against the Spirit. If we let our guard down, the enemy will take the chance to try to reignite the appetites of the flesh that once burned strong in our lives. The flesh will always try to re-establish itself in the life of every believer. This is not something we need to fear, but as believers need to walk in a spirit of wisdom and understand the need to be aware of the appetites of the flesh and be ready to deny them.

TAKE UP HIS CROSS.

If denying self wasn't big enough, Jesus then took the statement to the next level. We must follow, we must deny, and we then must take up **OUR CROSS.**

As New Testament believers we have the benefit of understanding this in the light of Christs sacrifice for us upon the cross of Calvary. But when Jesus spoke this to His disciples it was pre-crucifixion! Think how extreme this must have sounded. Jesus disciples would have understood just what was meant by the cross. They were familiar with this act of Roman cruelty. The cross was a death sentence, there was no surviving it. The cross was where criminals and those guilty of transgressing the law were sentenced. It was a horrible, gruesome way to die.

The call of Jesus was not to die on the cross though, it was to take up and carry our crosses! Jesus carried His cross and we are called to do the same. It is to carry that sentence of death, to take up that which symbolises death in the flesh. To pick up your cross, is to lay down your life. In taking up His cross, Jesus was laying down His rights to His life. The call for us to take up our cross is to do the same. It takes the act of denying the flesh one step further. To take up our cross is to lay down our claim to our life. It's a declaration to the Lord that this life I lay down for you to use. It is an act of sacrifice.

It's not enough for us as believers to just deny the flesh we have to die to the flesh as well. **DENYING** says no, but **DYING TO** removes the flesh completely. As we take up our cross, we die to the flesh.

AND FOLLOW ME.

Having taken up our cross, we are then to follow Jesus. We literally carry our cross as we look unto Jesus and follow Him in His footsteps. As mentioned earlier, notice that it doesn't mention that we die upon our cross! After taking up our cross, we carry it, and we follow Him. It is a life of sacrifice. A continuing journey of living for Him whilst we are here on the earth. It is a life that has put self aside and is focused on the Spirit. It is a life that has laid itself down and chosen to follow Him. We deny, we take up (die) and we follow.

Deny → Take Up (Die) → Follow

In this verse from Matthew Jesus describes for us a completely surrendered life. It is a life that lives for Him and not for self. It is a life that lays everything else down to follow Him. It is a life that denies and dies to self in order to follow Him wholeheartedly. To follow is to give our lives to His service.

What Jesus describes for us here is beautifully illustrated in terms of worship in the life of Abraham's son, Isaac. Isaac was the long awaited for son of promise for Abraham. When Isaac was in his teenage years, the Lord came to Abraham and asked him to sacrifice his son of promise unto the Lord. Abraham without hesitation immediately set out to do this in complete obedience unto the Lord. After a journey of three days Abraham, Isaac and their servants arrived at the place God had spoken to Abraham about. Leaving the servants behind, Abraham and Isaac set off and in Genesis 22 we read:

> *So **Abraham took the wood of the burnt offering and laid it on Isaac his son**; and he took the fire in his hand, and a knife, and the two of them went together. But Isaac spoke to Abraham his father and said, "My father!" And he said, "Here I am, my son." Then he said, "Look, the fire and the wood, but where is the lamb for a burnt offering?" And Abraham said, "My son, God will provide for Himself the lamb*

> *for a burnt offering." So the two of them went together. Then they came to the place of which God had told him. And Abraham built an altar there and placed the wood in order; and he bound Isaac his son and laid him on the altar, upon the wood. (Gen 22:6-9) NKJV*

Abraham acted in complete obedience unto the word of the Lord unto him. Isaac, the long-awaited son of promise, was to be a burnt offering unto the Lord! In order to fulfill this command Abraham made an altar out of wood upon which to offer his son. A sacrifice required an altar! This altar was made from the very wood that Isaac had carried up the hill. Isaac had literally carried his cross up the hill. Abraham then bound his son and laid him on the altar. Whilst we generally focus in on the faith of Abraham in this passage and wonder how a father could ever trust the Lord this much, we must also take into account the faith of Isaac. Isaac was at an age where he could have resisted and fought his elderly father. He did not have to comply with this! He could have gotten off the altar! He could have questioned, he could have argued, but he didn't! In this worship unto the Lord, Isaac denied himself, took up his cross and surrendered completely to the will of his father. It is such a prophetic act of not only the sacrifice of Jesus, but also of what each and every believer is called to do. We are to deny self, we are to take up our cross and we are to follow Him in obedience to the will of the Father. This is to worship in spirit.

What we see through Jesus words and Isaacs example is an attitude of sacrifice. We follow after Him, taking up our cross and dyeing to self. But before we can take up our cross, we must first deny self. It is only when we have **DENIED SELF** that we can then **DIE TO SELF**. This dying to self is what is required in our worship if we are to fulfil the standard of worship in spirit. In order to worship in spirit the flesh has to be completely removed, it has to be died to. We deny, we take up our cross and we follow.

Through Jesus words and Isaacs example we see a beautiful picture of how we as believers are to respond in order to die to the flesh and worship in spirit. We see here an act of sacrifice described by Jesus for those who follow the Lord. When we come to the book of Romans, we see this very same thought expanded and explained in greater detail by the apostle Paul.

Living Sacrifices

In Romans 12 Paul makes an impassioned plea to his readers in regard to how they were to live:

> *I beseech you therefore, brethren, by the mercies of God, that you present your bodies a living sacrifice, holy, acceptable to God, which is your reasonable service. (Rom 12:1) NKJV*

Paul was brought up as a Pharisee and had an amazing knowledge of the Old Testament. This was a gift that the Lord used to bring the truths of the Old Testament through to New Testament believers. In this verse, Paul under the inspiration of the Holy Spirit was applying Old Testament understanding in regard to the sacrificial system and its operation to New Testament believers. For us to understand the fulness of what Paul was saying here we need to break this verse down and examine its parts.

THE ROLES OF SACRIFICE.

Paul started off by imploring believers to present their bodies as a living sacrifice.

> *I beseech you therefore, brethren, by the mercies of God, that you present* **your bodies a living sacrifice**, ... *(Rom 12:1) NKJV*

Within this simple statement Paul links two separate and individual roles that are essential for sacrifice, the role of priest and the role of sacrifice. In the Old Testament these two roles were completely distinct, but under the inspiration of the Spirit, Paul unites the two in reference to believers. Paul takes the role of priest and the role of sacrifice and states that both of these apply to New Testament believers!

The Priestly Role.

> *that you* **present** *your bodies a living sacrifice. Rom 12:1 (NKJV)*

Under the Old Testament economy, the priestly role belonged to Aaron and his sons who were of the tribe of Levi. They were the ones chosen by God to **PRESENT** His offerings upon the altar. The people would bring their sacrifices and offerings unto the priests at the Tabernacle and Temple, and it was then that the priests would **PRESENT** the sacrifices unto the Lord on behalf of the people. They were the middlemen. The priests were the ones to present the sacrifices before the Lord.

Under the New Testament economy, we understand that we as believers are priests unto the Lord under our Great High Priest, Jesus.

> *But you are a chosen generation,* **a royal priesthood***, a holy nation, His own special people, that you may proclaim the praises of Him who called you out of darkness into His marvelous light; (1Pe 2:9) NKJV*

> *And hast* **made us unto our God kings and priests***: and we shall reign on the earth. (Rev 5:10) KJV*

It is to this role that Paul is referring. Believers are priests under Jesus. Just as the Levitical priests served under Aaron, so to do believers serve under Jesus. As believer priests' part of our role is to serve the Lord and present sacrifices unto Him. That is what Paul was calling us to do. He was calling us to present a sacrifice unto the Lord. As priests that is our role, our call, our obligation and our duty. We are to present unto the Lord.

The Sacrificial Role.

> *that you present* **your bodies** *a living sacrifice. Rom 12:1 (NKJV)*

Whilst Paul called us to present a sacrifice as priests, he also said in the same breath that the sacrifice we are to present is our bodies. As believer priests we are to present ourselves unto the Lord. In this sense we are both the offeror and the offering. We fulfill the roles of

Abraham and Isaac, the priest and the sacrifice. As priests we present ourselves as the offering.

A sacrifice is something unmistakably linked to death and that is the essence of what Paul is imploring his readers to. He is imploring them to lay down their lives, take up their cross, offer themselves upon the altar and die to the flesh. If we reflect on our example of Abraham and Isaac, we see Isaac's cross was also his altar! It was one and the same thing. Isaac took up his cross and presented himself on this altar unto the Lord. Paul is imploring his readers that as New Testament priests we are to present our lives upon the altar and unto the Lord in sacrifice.

The sacrifice we present though is not a normal sacrifice, it is a living sacrifice. As priests we are called to present our lives unto Him as a living sacrifice. But what is a living sacrifice? The very thought seems contradictory! A living sacrifice though is exactly what Jesus was talking about when He said to take up our cross and follow Him. A living sacrifice sacrifices itself unto the Lord that it may live for Him and not for self. This means that our lives are not our own, but rather they are His, given to Him by us in sacrifice. It is a dying to the flesh and everything that the flesh would desire and living simply and wholly for Him. In the fullest since when we present ourselves as living sacrifices, we fulfill the words of Jesus when He taught His disciples to pray:

> ***Your*** *Kingdom come.* ***Your will*** *be done, in earth as it is in Heaven. (Mat 6:10) KJV*

It is only when self has been offered as a living sacrifice that we can truly utter these words. This is exactly what Paul was talking about. We live to serve Him and His will. In presenting ourselves as living sacrifices, the flesh is removed, it is sacrificed upon the altar, and we live to serve sacrificially. We are living sacrifices, wholly dedicated unto the Lord and His will, living by the Spirit because the flesh has been dealt with. As living sacrifices, we daily carry our cross and present ourselves unto Him for His will to be done.

THE REQUIREMENTS OF SACRIFICE.

Holy, acceptable unto God. Rom 12:1 (NKJV)

Whilst we have seen that there are two distinct roles of sacrifice, we also need to understand that both of these roles had their own God given requirements for the sacrifice to be accepted. There were requirements upon both the priests who were to offer and also upon the sacrifice that was to be offered. To understand the ramifications of this we need to understand what made the priest holy and acceptable and what made the sacrifice holy and acceptable.

As Priests.

Holy and acceptable. Rom 12:1 (NKJV)

We have already discussed that in this verse Paul is referring to the Old Testament economy to explain a New Testament truth. In particular Paul is referring to the Tabernacle system that was introduced with the Tabernacle of Moses. This was where the priestly offices and their responsibility for the sacrifices were first introduced to the nation of Israel.

At the Tabernacle of Moses all sacrifice occurred in the area known as the Outer Court and within this area there were two pieces of furniture that have particular application to what we are discussing. These are the Brazen Altar and the Brazen Laver.

The Brazen Altar was the largest piece of tabernacle furniture and was made from wood overlaid with brass. Brass in scripture speaks of the Lord's judgment against sin. It was this very thing that occurred at the Brazen Altar as it was the place of sacrifice. It was here and here alone that the blood was shed, and the sacrifices were presented. The Brazen Altar was an altar of blood. It was here that the innocent substitute victims were offered as a means of atonement for the people of Israel.

The Brazen Laver was similarly located in the Outer Court and was also made out of bronze. In fact, scripture tells us that the

Brazen Laver was made from the looking glasses of the women of Israel. These were pieces of brass that had been polished to such a degree that one's reflection could be seen in them. Such speaks to the introspection that this article of furniture is associated with. The Brazen Laver was filled with water and was a place of washing.

When priests first came into service these two pieces of furniture played an important role. In Leviticus 8 at the dedication of Aaron and his sons, we read of these two elements being involved in their consecration to ministry into the role of the priesthood. We see in these two elements the representation of blood and water, sacrifice and washing. Such speaks to us as New Testament Christians of salvation and baptism. When we accept Jesus as our savour and receive His sacrifice for us, we are washed in His blood and then we receive baptism into His name, being washed in His water. When we enter into our priesthood, we experience the same thing as Aaron and his sons! We attend the altar, and we attend the laver.

Whilst we see that these two pieces are involved in the initiation of the priestly office, we go on to discover that the Brazen Laver played a continual role in the lives of the priests. In Exodus we read:

> *When they go into the tabernacle of meeting, or when they come near the altar to minister, to burn an offering made by fire to the LORD,* **they shall wash with water***, lest they die. So* **they shall wash their hands and their feet, lest they die.** *And it shall be a statute forever to them—to him and his descendants throughout their generations." (Exo 30:20-21)*
> NKJV

Whenever the priests came unto the Tabernacle of Moses to minister, whether it was to go into the Tent of Meeting, to the Table of Shewbread, The Golden Lampstand etc or whether it was remaining in the Outer Court and ministering at the Brazen Altar with the burnt offerings, they had to visit the Brazen Laver. On any given day, before a priest could minister, they visited the Brazen Laver and washed.

The Brazen Laver speaks of both reflection or self-inspection and washing. In terms of reflection or self-inspection we see that the Brazen Laver was made of brass that came from the looking glasses of the women of Israel (Gen 38:8). We noted above that this was brass that had been polished to a point that one's own reflection was now visible. Such highlights the association of self-reflection with the brazen laver. The priests would attend the laver and examine themselves before they proceeded to operate in their office. This was a preparatory act before they would operate in their priestly function.

For us as believers this speaks of the need to examine ourselves before we step into our priestly role. It is possibly with this thought in mind that Jesus tells us in Matt 5 that if we remember our brother has something against us, leave our gift and the altar and sort that out before continuing (Matt 5:23-24). There is a need for us to be right on the inside before we serve. It is an act of preparation before operation.

In terms of washing, we discovered that the laver was filled with water. As mentioned above, at the time of their ordination the priests would wash in the water of the laver before they stepped into their office. Such speaks of the baptism of the saints when we come to Jesus. It is once we accept Jesus as our Lord and Saviour and are baptised that we become part of the Priesthood of all believers.

After this ordination though, the Priests would then regularly come to the laver and wash, before they would minister for that day (Ex 30:17-21).

Whilst the priests of the Old Testament had been "baptised" they were still required by the Lord to wash in order to be holy. The same truth applies to us as New Testament believers. Whilst we have been baptised, on a daily basis we still need to attend the Brazen Laver and honestly inspect ourselves and be washed in the water of the Word of the Lord. Note in particular what parts of the body the Lord instructs the priests to wash in Exodus:

> *So they shall wash **their hands and their feet**, that they die not: and it shall be a statute for ever to them, even to him and to his seed throughout their generations. (Exo 30:20-21) KJV*

The priests were to regularly wash their hands and their feet. It was not a complete bath, just their hands and their feet. Our feet speak of our walk, how we have lived and conducted ourselves. Our hands speak of our actions, what we have or haven't done. Having been baptised as believers we don't need to be completely rewashed on a daily basis, but we do need to examine our walk and actions and wash accordingly. This thought is touched on by Jesus in John 13:1-10 when Peter refused to let Jesus wash his feet:

> *Jesus said to him, "**He who is bathed needs only to wash his feet**, but is completely clean; and you are clean, but not all of you." (Joh 13:10) NKJV*

Before the priests could be holy and acceptable and offer the sacrifices required of them, they had to attend the Brazen Laver. **WASHING PRECEEDED OFFERING**. Preparation of self was required in order to be able to minister unto the Lord. The priests were called, but they still had to prepare themselves through washing before they could function in their role unto the Lord. Every time they came to serve, they washed.

Such speaks of the need for believers to daily wash themselves in the Word of God, cleansing from every spot of sin. After being ordained as priests, the priests would then only wash their hands and their feet. The priests did not need to be re-baptised; they just needed their actions, and their walk cleansed from any errors they had made.

We read in scripture that the Word of God is compared to both water and a mirror that gives reflection (Eph 5:26 and Jam 1:22-23). For the New Testament believers, we are to wash in the Word and seek and allow the Holy Spirit to reveal those things that are in our lives that need to be attended to. It is when we wash in His Word, allowing His truth to wash us, and when we let the Holy Spirit inspect us through the truth of the Word, that we are made holy and acceptable. The truths of the Brazen Laver still apply!

The reality is all of us err in some way on any given day. We are all being perfected but none of us are yet perfect. We don't need to be re-baptised though, but just as the priests of the Old Testament, we need to wash our hands and our feet, our actions and our walk. This is what Jesus was saying. We don't need to re-bathe, we have been washed, we just need to have our hands and feet attended to. This is the preparatory act we undertake before coming before the Lord. Such is a recognition that we are coming before a Holy God.

<u>As Sacrifices</u>.

Holy and acceptable. Rom 12:1 (NKJV)

One only has to read through the book of Leviticus to understand that the Lord had very clear standards for what was holy and acceptable in terms of sacrifice. The people could not just bring whatever they wanted, there was a Godly standard that had to be met. One of the overarching requirements was that the sacrifice had to be **without blemish**. God had divine standards that He expected His people to uphold. Not just anything would do.

In order for the Israelites to make sure that their sacrifices measured up, they needed to inspect them well before they ever got to the altar. It was not a case of bring the sacrifice and see if the priest thinks it is acceptable. The responsibility lay upon the people to make sure that what they were going to bring met the requirements that the Lord had laid out.

In other words, before the sacrifice was brought the people had to prepare. They had to inspect, they had to check, they had to make sure that what they were going to bring would be accepted by the Lord. Sacrifice took preparation to ensure it meet the Lord's requirements.

Israel though did not always adhere to this. Note the words of the Lord in Malachi:

> *"A son honors his father, And a servant his master. If then I am the Father, Where is My honor? And if I am a Master, Where is My reverence? Says the LORD of hosts To you priests who despise My name. Yet you say, 'In what way have we despised Your name?'" "You offer defiled food on My altar, But say, 'In what way have we defiled You?' By saying, 'The table of the LORD is contemptible.'* **And when you offer the blind as a sacrifice, Is it not evil? And when you offer the lame and sick, Is it not evil? Offer it then to your governor! Would he be pleased with you? Would he accept you favorably?" Says the LORD of hosts.** *"But now entreat God's favor, That He may be gracious to us. While this is being done by your hands, Will He accept you favorably?" Says the LORD of hosts. (Mal 1:6-9) NKJV*

The people of Israel were keeping the appearance of religion, but their heart was far from it. What they would not dare give unto man for fear of reproach and embarrassment, they were more than happy to give unto the Lord. They brought unto the Lord a "sacrifice", but it was not what the Lord required. The Lord had clear guidelines for what was holy and acceptable in terms of sacrifice and anything inferior to this was not counted as acceptable. It was in fact an insult and in no way honoured the Lord. It is only when we bring a holy and acceptable sacrifice, according to the divine standard, that we honour the Lord.

Romans tells us that we present ourselves as a living sacrifice upon the altar. Just as there were requirements upon the Old Testament sacrifices so likewise are there standards and requirements with New Testament worship. The message of the Lord through Paul is that we are to present ourselves **HOLY AND ACCEPTABLE** unto the Lord. We can't just turn up and presume we are holy and acceptable; we need to prepare ourselves before we present ourselves to ensure we meet the Godly standard of being holy and acceptable. It is a preparatory task that precedes worship. Preparation precedes presentation. Before we present, we prepare.

Preparation Precedes Presentation

As living sacrifices, our bodies are what we present. Now that may sound fairly straight forward, but if we break it down a little and apply the standard of being holy and acceptable without any blemish, we start to see some things that are not immediately obvious. It is when we break down the body that we see just how all-encompassing that this statement is. Let's for a moment consider what makes up our bodies:

1) Our Mind.

> Our mind consists of our thoughts, what we think, and what we have thought.
> What has our mind dwelt on this week? Have we taken captive every thought and made it obedient to Christ?

2) Our Eyes.

> What we see, what we watch.
> What we have watched, what we have seen? What has been let in through our eye gate?

3) Our Ears.

> What we listen to, what we have heard, what we have chosen to listen to.
> What has come through our ear gate and lodged? What have we chosen to listen to?

4) Our Mouth.

> Our words, what we speak, what we have spoken.
> Have we spoken life or death, blessing or cursing? Are our lips clean in His sight?

5) Our Heart.

   Our attitudes, hopes, dreams, motives.
   What has taken root and what needs to be removed?

6) Our Hands.

   Our actions, that which we have done.
   What have we done throughout the week?

7) Our Feet.

   Our walk. How have we lived and conducted ourselves in the last week?
   Have we been faithful and true ambassadors of Christ in the world? What has the world seen this week in our walk?

As an Israelite one would never just assume that their offering was without blemish, it would have to be inspected. The sacrifice would be gone over to make sure that it met the Lord's divine standards, and this would happen well before it was brought unto the Lord to be presented. Preparation was required before sacrifice. If this was a standard to which the people of God were held under the Old Covenant which was but a shadow, how much more is it applicable to us as New Testament believers? We cannot just assume there is no blemish when we present ourselves, we have to inspect ourselves to make sure that we meet the requirements of being holy and acceptable and must occur well before we present ourselves otherwise, we risk receiving the same rebuke of the Lord that the people of Israel did in Malachi.

Hopefully through what we have looked at in these points, we have been able to highlight to that there is a Biblical standard that the Lord has for both his priests and his offerings to be holy and acceptable. Scripture clearly details this for us. If we are to fulfill both of these roles as Paul calls us to, then we need to be holy and acceptable.

As a sacrifice we need to inspect ourselves to see that we are without spot and blemish and if we are not then we need to deal with it. As priests we are to avail ourselves of the Brazen Laver, introspecting and being cleansed. It is when we do these things, that we are then holy and acceptable.

THE REASON FOR SACRIFICE.

*Which is **your reasonable service**. (Rom 12:1) NKJV*

Paul sums up his exhortation to believers by telling us that to present ourselves as a living sacrifice is our reasonable service. We present ourselves as living sacrifices, holy and acceptable because it is our reasonable service! The Greek word for reasonable as used here is 'logikos' and means "rational, logical". The reason we present and sacrifice ourselves is because it is our logical service. Given everything that Christ Jesus has done for us, it only makes sense that we present ourselves as a living sacrifice, holy and acceptable. For every believer that has accepted Jesus as their Lord and saviour, this is our reasonable, logical and I would go as far to say expected, service. Anything less is not befitting for our King.

In our previous example we saw the necessity to die to self and follow Jesus as we considered His words when He said "Take up your cross and follow me". In Romans we read of the same truth again, this time through the apostle Paul. As believers we are called to present ourselves as a living sacrifice unto the Lord. We are to offer ourselves unto Him, laying down our lives for His service. Paul though expands on this aspect of taking up our cross. In order to take up our cross and offer ourselves as a living sacrifice, we need to be holy and acceptable as both priest and offering. We have to attend to this before we can present. Preparation precedes presentation! Having prepared ourselves, we then present ourselves, taking up our cross and following Him.

Expanding upon this thought, I would put forth the following for your consideration. It is my belief that the imploration of Paul here was not in regard to a once off event. It is not a once off act of taking up our cross, but rather it is a lifestyle that Paul is calling believers to live by. I would suggest that Paul is actually encouraging a daily lifestyle observation for believers. Daily we are to die to the flesh, presenting ourselves as a holy and acceptable living sacrifice unto the Lord. We are to daily prepare ourselves as living sacrifices and take up our crosses. Every day that we are upon this earth we are to be a living sacrifice unto Him.

We have seen how the language used by Paul in this passage is a clear reference to the Old Testament economy and in particular the Tabernacle of Moses. One of the foundations of the Tabernacle system was the daily sacrifices that were performed every morning and every evening. These were regular sacrifices that occurred each and every single day of the year. Every morning there was a sacrifice and every evening there was sacrifice according to the commandment of the Lord.

My belief is that this is exactly what Paul was encouraging his readers to do. Sacrifice marked the start of the day and sacrifice marked the conclusion of the day. At both points of dawn and dusk God was front and centre. I would suggest that this is to be exactly the same with us as New Testament believers. Our bodies, our lives are to be living sacrifices presented to the Father **DAILY**. It is a life of sacrifice that we are called to live. We are to be daily in His service. Whilst we are to take up our cross and follow Him, the taking up of our cross is to be a daily event. Every day we are to die to the flesh, presenting our bodies as living sacrifices holy and acceptable unto Him. It is a daily function that we are to perform. It is a daily death to the flesh to live by the Spirit. When we die to the flesh, we are able to worship in spirit.

Daily we deny
Daily we take up
Daily we prepare ourselves
Daily we present ourselves
Daily we follow

What it looks like

So far in this section we have noted that in order to be able to worship in spirit we must first die to the flesh. We have then gone on to look at two scriptural examples, with the words of both Jesus and Paul, in regard to how we as believers do this. Having discovered the need to deal with the flesh in order to be able to worship in spirit the question that remains is what does worship in spirit look like.

In 2 Samuel 6:13-23 we read of David bringing up the Ark of the Lord to be placed in the Tabernacle of David:

> *Then* **David danced before the LORD with all his might**; *and David was wearing a linen ephod.* **So David and all the house of Israel brought up the ark of the LORD with shouting and with the sound of the trumpet.** *Now as the ark of the LORD came into the City of David, Michal, Saul's daughter, looked through a window and saw* **King David leaping and whirling before the LORD**; *and she despised him in her heart. (2Sa 6:14-16)*
> NKJV

We can observe here that David did a number of things when bringing the Ark of the Lord up:

1. David danced with all his might

    David was leaping or whirling, dancing before the Lord. David danced with all his might. Might is defined by Strongs as "*strength* in various applications *(force, security, majesty, praise)* and is translated as boldness, loud, might, power, strength, strong".

    David danced with all his might, all his strength, with everything that he had. He gave it all.

2. David shouted.

    David's body was active and so was his voice. His voice was shouting unto the Lord. He declared the truths of who His God was.

3. David responded to the sound of the trumpet.

   His ears were active and attentive. He was listening to the sound of the musicians and responding.

4. David leapt.

   Not just dancing but leaping before the Lord. David jumped for joy and gave of his energy and strength.

5. David danced before the Lord.

   David danced before the Lord. We can often assume that David must have been a good dancer, but we aren't actually told that. We are just told that he danced, and he did so with a focus of doing it before the Lord.

As we read these points, we may be tempted to think that these actions define what worship in spirit is. We can look at the actions of David above and admire the Spirit led nature of David's worship. The fact is though that the actions detailed above **DO NOT** define what worship in spirit is. These actions alone don't tell us that Davids worship was in spirit. These are not the definitions for worship in Spirit.

Earlier in this passage we are told that when David's first wife Michal looked down from her window and saw David dancing, she despised him in her heart. Once Davd returned home from this joyous day, Michal came out to meet him. She did not come in delight or with encouragement though, Michal came out and rebuked David for his actions: "How could a king act in such a fashion?" Note David's response though.

> *"**It was before the LORD**, who chose me instead of your father and all his house, to appoint me ruler over the people of the LORD, over Israel. Therefore I will play music before the LORD. **And I will be even more undignified than this, and will be humble in my own sight** But as for the maidservants of whom you have spoken, by them I will be held in honor." (2Sa 6:20-22) NKJV*

We see in this response the heart behind the worship of David. David's words to his wife were, "it was before the Lord that I did this". In other words, "I am in no way concerned with what man may or may not think about how I worship when I am worshipping the Lord". It did not bother David what the people thought, nor what his wife thought for that matter, for they were not the motivation for his actions. The only focus of David was the Lord. There was absolutely no concern for the flesh with David. Not with Michal and not with the people. David's worship was before the Lord.

Notice what David then goes on to say, "***And I will yet be more undignified than this, and will be humble in mine own sight***". In other translations this verse reads; "**I will be more base**"; "**I will be more contemptable**"; "**I will be more vile**". David was not concerned with his appearance in worship, his focus was solely and completely on the Lord. He was worshipping in Spirit because he was a man after God's own heart. The flesh had been dealt with, and David sought the Lord without the restrictions of the flesh.

Whilst this passage ends with David stating that the maid servants Michal had mentioned would see his worship and hold him in honour, we need to understand here that David wasn't looking for honour or worshipping for honour. David's motivation wasn't I did this to be honoured, his motivation was to worship the Lord, but he understood that the people would recognise and honour true worship. Why? Because worship in Spirit is so distinctly different to worship in the flesh and true worshippers will recognise true worship! Worship in flesh will always look to exalt self, whereas worship in spirit will always have a reverence for the Lord.

David's worship was vibrant and exuberant, but that is not what made it worship in spirit. We can imitate the acts of David and still worship in the flesh. What sets David's worship apart as worship in spirit is the **HEART** attitude behind it. What I do, I do before the Lord with no concern for how I am perceived. The balance to this comes in our next section on worship in truth, but for now what we need to grasp hold of is the heart attitude of David. David's worship was not dictated to by the opinions of man, it was wholly and completely in Spirit. The flesh had been died to. David had taken up his cross and presented himself as a living sacrifice unto the Lord, holy and acceptable. David worshipped in spirit.

Summary

At the start of this section we noted that in order to be able to worship in spirit we have to have removed all elements of the flesh. The flesh has to be dealt with by taking up our cross and following Jesus after the example of Isaac.

What we also noted that Paul is Galatians tells us how the flesh and the Spirit battle against one another. They are literally at war in our bodies and the fact of the matter is that as long as we are in our mortal bodies that battle will continue. Our Sprit may get stronger and our flesh weaker, but without continual attention this will not always remain the case. Any time we neglect the Spirit we allow the flesh to grow. That is where the words of Paul in Romans become so pertinent. The flesh has to be dealt with daily. It is how we sustain the victory. It is how we walk in the Spirit. It is how we worship in spirit. We need to take up our cross daily, presenting ourselves as living sacrifices, holy and acceptable.

In order to worship in spirit, we have to have a lifestyle of dealing with the flesh. It is the only way that we can meet the standard of true. Whenever we are coming before the Lord in worship we have to have already presented ourselves as a living sacrifice, having taken the time to make sure that as both the priest and the offering we are holy and acceptable. The preparation is just as important as the process. It is when we attend to the call of Jesus and Paul, having died to the flesh that we can truly worship in spirit. We prepare before we worship. There is no other way. It is only when we have completely died to self that we can truly, fully and completely focus in on God in true worship. When we have dealt with the flesh, we can then worship in spirit.

PREPARATION PRECEDES PRESENTATION.

Identifying the Flesh in our Worship.

Having spent some time examining scriptural examples of worship in the flesh and worship in spirit, and looking at the differences between them, we will now consider some points that can help us to identify worship that may be in flesh in our lives and in our Churches. The battle between flesh and Spirit is continual, but if we are to worship in spirit and meet the standard of true, the flesh has to be dealt with.

Again, this is not written to be condemnatory in nature, but as we discovered in our previous section, we need to be to open and honest enough to self-reflect and allow the Holy Spirit to reveal things to us that need to be dealt with if we are truly going to worship in spirit. What is presented is not an extensively check list, but rather things that have been impressed upon my spirit by the Lord as I prayed over and contemplated this matter. These are things that the I have had to examine within myself as I have sought to grow in the area of true worship.

With that being said, lets examine some things that can indicate to us that our worship may have fleshly elements that need to be dealt with.

Over Exuberance

The question may be asked, how can over exuberance in worship be a bad thing? If we are following the example of David and dancing, singing, shouting etc how can that indicate that flesh may be involved in our worship? What we need to remember is that it was not the actions of David that showed us that his worship was being performed in spirit, but rather it was his heart attitude. It always comes back to the focus of the heart.

In terms of over exuberance in worship the same truth applies. In considering our own worship an important question that we have to ask ourselves is whether we are worshipping for example or whether we are worshipping by example? It is the distinction between these two approaches that highlights to us whether the flesh is involved in what we are doing.

Worshipping for example is rooted in good motives. It seeks to set the example of how worship should be performed in an effort to encourage other believers to step out of their selves and fully embrace the Lord in their worship. In other words, "I am going to show everyone just how they should be worshipping." The problem with this though is that when we worship for example:

OUR FOCUS IN WORSHIP SHIFTS.

Rather than our focus being solely on the Lord, it is on making sure that those who are observing us are seeing what worship should look like. Our actions are not done solely unto the Lord, our worship is done that man might see. Whilst the intentions for this may be good in nature, part of our motivation in worship has actually become focused on man. Our worship can almost become performance orientated as it seeks to impress man with an amazing display. We become more intent on what we are doing in worship than we are on the one we are supposed to be worshipping.

THE FOCUS OF OTHERS SHIFTS.

When we are worshipping for example, we are actually expecting that some of the focus of others in worship will be on us. We are presuming to take the attention due unto God and direct it unto ourselves. Sometimes the extent of our worship is such a distraction that individuals lose focus of God altogether as we become the primary focus. Unintentionally we are wanting others to focus on us in worship rather than the Lord.

Whenever we worship for example, we introduce flesh into not only our worship, but also to the worship of others. Whilst our intentions may be good, we actually hinder ourselves and others in pursuing God in spirit. When we worship for example, we become the centre of attention, and the Lord becomes a bystander.

On the other hand, when we worship by example, we follow in the footsteps of king David. When we worship by example, our worship may be just as exuberant as those that worship for example, but, and this is the key, like David we are focused solely and completely on the Lord. We are not focused on the thoughts of others good or bad, we are focused solely on the Lord most high. We are not focused on showing others how to worship, we are completely and solely focused on bringing unto the Lord the worship He deserves.

The difference is that when we worship for example, we are conscious of the focus being on us, whereas when we worship by example, we are conscious of the focus being solely and completely on God. Over exuberance is not necessarily bad, it just depends on the heart motivation for it. Why are we doing it? What is our motivation? We can never worship for anyone else; we should only ever worship for Him.

Under Exuberance

At the other extreme, under exuberance in worship is usually a clear sign that the flesh is involved in our worship. The worship that David offered should actually be the normal worship for each and every one of us! For some of us when we read that statement it may seem rather challenging. But the fact of the matter is that spirit led exuberance in worship is normal. If we are finding that hard, we have to ask the question why? If we are completely honest, the general response would be that there are certain things that we may feel uncomfortable doing in public. We may not be the best singers, we may have two left feet, we may not have any rhythm. In other words, we are afraid of how we will look in the sight of others! The fear of man is a stronghold of the flesh that will hinder us from being able to worship in spirit.

The fact of the matter is that we do not know that David was a good dancer, a good singer or if he had rhythm. We assume so because of his worship and his psalms, but we do not know that. He may have been terrible! Whether this was true or not, David was never hindered in his worship by his abilities or lack thereof. Why? Because he did it unto the Lord, not unto man. It didn't matter what man thought, David's focus was on the Lord.

If people are looking at us in worship, then their focus is off, but we can't let it affect ours. Just as David was unfazed by Michal, so to do we need to have a boldness that shakes off the fear of man and follow the leading of the Holy Spirit in worship. We are to dance, to jump, to sing, to clap all as the Spirit leads us as we worship unto the Lord. It is when we die to the flesh that we can fully embrace this.

An Over Emphasis on Praise

Praise is in integral part of our worship, but it is not the only part of worship, and it certainly is not the totality of worship. Praise is important, but it is not all important. In modern Church, and indeed in the lives of believers, there can be an overemphasis on praise which stems from three things: a misunderstanding of what praise actually is, a misunderstanding of what praise does for God and a misunderstanding of what praise does for us.

As we look at each of these points individually, what we will see is that all of these misunderstandings actually have their roots in the flesh.

A MISUNDERSTANDING OF WHAT PRAISE ACTUALLY IS.

Today praise is generally defined as music that is loud, upbeat and engaging. One of the key factors in a lot of Church services is for the praise to attract and engage the people in worship. The problem with this though is that when we are looking for the music to engage people, we are actually appealing to the flesh. When we talk about praise being engaging, what we are actually saying is that the flesh of people is drawn in because they like what they are hearing. If people's engagement is the motivation for the praise that we sing in our services, then all we are doing is enabling the flesh in our services rather than cultivating Spirit lead worship. Praise is not about engaging people. It is not about engaging the flesh. Praise has absolutely nothing to do with us whatsoever.

The writer of Hebrews tells us:

> *Therefore by Him let us **continually offer the sacrifice of praise to God**, that is, the fruit of our lips, giving thanks to His name. (Heb 13:15) NKJV*

Praise is meant to be sacrificial in nature and as we have already looked at in this section, by definition sacrifice means dying to the flesh. We therefore cannot look to engage the flesh in praise, when praise by definition is meant to involve death to the flesh. We have it mixed up because our understanding of praise is off.

Praise is not about the music being loud, upbeat, engaging or modern. Those things have absolutely nothing to do with praise. Praise may be upbeat, but it doesn't have to be! Praise may be loud, but it doesn't have to be! Praise at its most basic definition is an act that declares the truths of God and expresses our thanks to Him (Ps 50:23). This can be loud, it can be quiet, it can be upbeat, or it can be slow. Praise is not limited to a musical style! Praise is far more than that.

Whilst we have to have an understanding of the musicality surrounding praise, we also need to have an understanding of the lyricality as well. In some modern praise there can be a general focus on self, which is just another way of engaging the flesh. Praise is actually meant to be more about God rather than about what we want God to do for us! It should be more 'Him' focused than 'I' focused. That which we declare should be focused on the truths surrounding God. It should be based on the truths of what scripture tells us about the Lord and who He is.

As believers though we can tend to be drawn to praise that engages our flesh and makes us feel better as we declare what God can do for us and immediately feel better about our life and circumstances. Praise though is not meant to satisfy self. It is not meant to satisfy the flesh; it is meant to kill it. That is why we are to offer the sacrifice of praise. The flesh has been dealt with, and we praise in Spirit.

Praise is not to meant to engage the flesh and nor is it meant to be the entirety of our worship. When all we do is praise because we enjoy it, praise actually becomes our idol, and God is not glorified. Praise is meant to be the starting point of our worship, not the fulness of it. Just as sacrifice was the starting point in the Tabernacle for the priests to approach unto the Lord, so too is praise. It is the starting point, but we are to progress past praise into worship and the presence of the Lord.

As believers we need to have a right understanding of what praise is. We need to have a Biblical definition of it and understand that if our flesh is being glorified in praise, then we are not offering true worship. The praise that we give is to have absolutely nothing to do in regard to how we feel when giving it. Our feelings in praise are actually somewhat irrelevant as it is supposed to be all about Him and how He is glorified as we offer the sacrifice of praise. As Paul said in Romans, this is our reasonable (logical) service!

A MISUNDERSTANDING OF WHAT PRAISE DOES FOR GOD.

> *But You are holy,* **Enthroned** *in the praises of Israel. (Psa 22:3) NKJV*

> *But thou art holy, O thou that* **inhabitest** *the praises of Israel. (Psa 22:3) KJV*

The misunderstanding about what praise does for the Lord is highlighted by a misinterpretation of the above verse. It is the misunderstanding of this verse that contributes to an over emphasis of praise in our services.

Some translation of Psalm 22:3, as the NKJV above, render the word 'inhabitest' to the word 'enthroned', which in our English understanding changes the verse to read that the Lord is enthroned on the praises of His people. Whilst a small change, this can actually change the whole context of how we read this verse. With this change this verse can be taken to mean that when we praise the Lord, we enthrone Him, therefore we should praise more and more enthusiastically so that the Lord is enthroned. Rather than being an action that God does in response to praise i.e. God inhabits, it becomes an action that man's praise accomplishes, i.e. it enthrones God.

There are however two problems with this. Firstly, the Lord is already enthroned (Rev 5:1, Heb 12:2, 10:12). He is seated in heaven! Our praises don't do that, He is already there enthroned. Jesus is already seated at the right hand of the Father! What praise does though is enthrone Him in our lives. When we praise, the things that the flesh has magnified and exalted are taken off the throne of our lives and God is reestablished there. As we declare the truths about the greatness of the Lord it realigns our spiritual man, reenthroning the Lord to his rightful place.

Secondly the Hebrew word that is interpreted as enthroned carries with it more the thought of someone coming and joining in fellowship with us. The better interpretation of this word is inhabits or dwell. When the word enthroned has been used, it is actually referring to God coming and sitting in our midst as we praise. This verse is about an action that God does in response to the praise of His people. When we praise, He comes and inhabits, dwells, sits in our presence. As we praise, His presence comes into our midst.

When we are praising, as part of our worship, what we are actually doing is bringing spiritual realignment into our inner man. When we praise, declaring the truths of who God is, we take our focus off the cares and problems of life that have consumed our thinking, and we place God as the central focus of our lives. Praise is the initiation point, it is the place of sacrifice, the first step in our approach unto the Lord. As we die to the flesh and praise in spirit, recorrecting our focus back onto the Lord, we invite Him into our midst. His presence meets us in response to our praise. As His presence comes and dwells in our praises, our praise should naturally move into worship. We move from a place of declaring the truths of God, to a place of reverence of His holiness. We move from the altar of sacrifice into the Most Holy Place and the presence of God.

Our praise does not enthrone the Lord, but it does invite Him to come and meet with us. It is not about the action of man, but the response of the Lord to the heart of man. For this to happen though we need to make sure that our definition of praise is in line with what scripture declares.

A MISUNDERSTANDING OF WHAT PRAISE DOES FOR US.

> *So the people shouted when the priests blew the trumpets. And it happened when the people heard the sound of the trumpet, and the people shouted with a great shout, that the wall fell down flat. Then the people went up into the city, every man straight before him, and they took the city. (Jos 6:20) NKJV*

On the seventh day, as the trumpets sounded and the people of Israel lifted up their voices and shouted, the walls of Jericho came crashing down. The account of Jericho is one that is used frequently in regard to the power that praise has. That which stood in resistance to the people of God was demolished as the people raised their voices. As we read this, our minds can immediately be drawn to the thought that praise brought the breakthrough. There is a truth to this, but I would suggest that it was not praise that brought the walls of Jericho down! It was not praise that brought the victory that day, but **OBEDIENCE**. To understand this more let us consider the whole account of what happened at Jericho by looking at Joshua chapters 6, 7 and 8. I would encourage you to take the time to read over these chapters before moving forward here.

IDENTIFYING THE FLESH IN OUR WORSHIP

In Joshua 6 the Lord came unto Joshua and declared that He had given into the hand of Joshua the city of Jericho, its king and all its valiant men. The Lord then laid out unto Joshua the process for how this would occur. For six days all the men of war were to march around the city accompanied by the priests with the Ark of the Lord. As they went around the city, seven priests were to blow their trumpets, but the people were to remain silent. For six days they were to do this, going around the city once each day. On the seventh day though, they were to compass the city seven times. After the seventh lap, when the people heard the priests make a long blast with the trumpets all the people were to shout and as they did, the cities walls would fall down flat.

This most likely was not the battle plan that Joshua had been pondering and was possibly not one he thought the army and people of Israel would respond well to. In faith though Joshua gave this word of the Lord to the priests, the army and the people. For six days Israel marched around the walls of Jericho, once each day with the Ark of the Lord and the seven priests with seven trumpets sounding while the people remained in complete silence. Then on the seventh day, after they had marched around the city seven times, the trumpets were sounded with a long blast, the people raised their voices and shouted, and the walls of Jericho fell down.

The key for us to understand in this is that the battle of Jericho was not won on **ONE** day, it took **SEVEN**! It was not praise that brought the victory, but faith and obedience unto the word of the Lord. Whilst the walls fell after the voices were lifted in a shout of praise, this was only because of the obedience that had **PRECEDED** this. As I was contemplating this thought, I was struck by the following questions:

Would the falls of Jericho have fallen:

- If the people of Israel had just gone straight to shouting on day one?

- If they had shouted on day two?

- If on day seven they had only compassed the city once and then shouted?
- If the Ark had never set out with the people of Israel as they marched around the city?
- If the priests never sounded the trumpets?
- If the soldiers didn't arm themselves as they marched?

Whilst possibly slightly excessive, what these questions hopefully highlight is that there was not one singular element that brought about the victory. We tend to focus on the shout of the praise because that was the last element before the walls fell, but the truth of the matter is that the silent march on the first day was just as important as the shout of praise on the seventh! The walls of Jericho fell because of the obedience of Joshua and the people of Israel unto the word of the Lord. It was not praise, but faithful obedience unto the Lord.

> ***By faith*** *the walls of Jericho fell down after* ***they were encircled for seven days****. (Heb 11:30) NKJV*

Faith at its core is belief and obedience unto the Word of the Lord. It is trusting God above all else. This is what Joshua and Israel did. As they magnified the Lord through their obedience unto His Word, that which seemed to be a strong hold lost its strength. As they walked in obedience unto the Lord, they received the blessing of the Lord. This is a truth we see revealed further as we continue reading in Joshua 7 and 8.

At the start of Chapter 7, we are told of the sin of Achan:

> *But the children of Israel committed a trespass regarding the accursed things, for Achan the son of Carmi, the son of Zabdi, the son of Zerah, of the tribe of Judah, took of the accursed things; so the anger of the LORD burned against the children of Israel. (Jos 7:1) NKJV*

It is interesting to note that whilst the anger of the Lord was kindled against the children of Israel, they seemed to be unaware of it. There was perhaps a lack of sensitivity to the presence of the Lord! Israel continued from the high of Jericho unaware that anything had changed.

The next battle that the Israelites were to face in the promised land was that of Ai. After the battle of Jericho, Joshua sent out men to spy out the region and report back to him. The men returned and reported unto Joshua that not all the men would need to go out in battle, just a few thousand would suffice. Note the confidence that had come upon the nation since the Lord had brought about the victory at Jericho! Compared to the stronghold of Jericho, this battle was supposed to be an easy one. It would only require a fraction of the strength of Israel.

Joshua heeded the advice of the spies and sent up about three thousand men in battle, but things did not go as planned:

> *So about three thousand men went up there from the people,* **but they fled before the men of Ai**. *And the men of Ai struck down about thirty-six men, for they chased them from before the gate as far as Shebarim, and struck them down on the descent; therefore the hearts of the people melted and became like water. (Jos 7:4-5) NKJV*

The victory did not come as planned! What started in faith and confidence ended in fear and trembling. In response to this defeat, Joshua rent his clothes and fell upon his face before the Ark of Lord. Joshua then poured out his complaint unto the Lord about why the Lord had let this happen and what it would mean for the Israelites moving forward.

The Lord's response was swift and sharp:

> *So the LORD said to Joshua:* **"Get up! Why do you lie thus on your face? Israel has sinned,** *and they have also transgressed My covenant which I commanded them. For they have even taken some of the accursed things, and have both stolen and deceived; and they have also put it among their own stuff.*

> ***Therefore*** *the children of Israel could not stand before their enemies, but turned their backs before their enemies, because they have become doomed to destruction. Neither will I be with you anymore, unless you destroy the accursed from among you. (Jos 7:10-12) NKJV*

Rather than answer the lament that Joshua had put forward, the Lord questioned him. Why are you on your face crying out to me when there is sin in the camp? You are looking in the wrong place! The Lord told Joshua that sin that had occurred and that this was the reason for their defeat. The Lord continued and told Joshua that unless this was dealt with, they would never be able to stand before their enemies. The Lord here brought Joshua back to the issue of Achan's sin (Jos 7:1). In obedience unto the command of the Lord, Joshua then investigated the matter and found that the sin lay with Achan. Joshua confronted Achan and Achan subsequently confessed his sin:

> *And Achan answered Joshua and said, "Indeed I have sinned against the LORD God of Israel, and this is what I have done: When I saw among the spoils a beautiful Babylonian garment, two hundred shekels of silver, and a wedge of gold weighing fifty shekels, I coveted them and took them. And there they are, hidden in the earth in the midst of my tent, with the silver under it." (Jos 7:20-21) NKJV*

The question we need to consider here is what was so significant about Achan taking these few items from Jericho? Why would the anger of the Lord have been raised because Achan took a few things from what would have been a massive plunder? The answer for us lies back in Joshua 6 when the Lord was laying out for Joshua the battle plan against Jericho:

> *And you, by all means abstain from the accursed things, lest you become accursed when you take of the accursed things, and make the camp of Israel a curse, and trouble it.* ***But all the silver and gold, and vessels of bronze and iron, are***

consecrated to the LORD; they shall come into the treasury of the LORD."(Jos 6:18-19) NKJV

That which was of the plunder of Jericho belonged unto the Lord. Everything that was found, all the silver, gold and brass was consecrated unto the Lord and was to be given unto Him. Jericho was the first city of the promised land. The spoils that came from the victory were the first fruits of what Israel was to receive and according to the law of the Lord these belonged unto Him. This was Israel's tithe! After the walls had fallen, Israel was to take that which they reaped from Jericho and dedicate it all unto the Lord as an act of worship. Israels obedience was to continue from praise to worship. When Achan's sinned though, God was robbed of the worship that was due to Him (Mal 3:6-8).

The reality of what we see here is that the praise that led to the walls of Jericho to fall was to lead to worship in the giving of the first fruits of the land unto the Lord. Praise was to lead to worship! The nation experienced the blessing of obedience when they were faithful in praise, but this blessing lifted when they were disobedient in worship! Their obedience was not to stop at praise, it was to continue into worship. As Israel walked in obedience there was to be a natural flow from praise to worship.

When the Israelites lifted their voices and blew their trumpets in an act of praise against the walls of Jericho, they were being obedient to the Word of God and in faith declaring that they believed that His Word was greater than the walls that stood before them. It was a sacrificial offering where they had to die to all that their eyes and mind were telling them, and raised their voices unto the Lord in complete belief of His Word to Joshua. It was a declaration that the truths of God were stronger than the walls that stood before them. It was a spiritual realignment as the Lord became bigger than that which stood before them.

As they in obedience did this, the Lord came and inhabited their praise, as we looked at in our previous point. As the Lord came and sat in the midst of their praise, that which was previously considered a stronghold was considered as nothing in the presence of the mighty

King. As they spiritually realigned themselves taking their focus off the issue at hand and turning unto the Lord, God came into their midst, and it was His tangible presence that should have lead them into worship. Praise sees us encounter His presence, but it is always to lead to worship. Worship should be the natural result of encountering the presence of God.

With Jericho we see that obedience is the overarching theme. The Israelites were obedient to the Word of the Lord and obedient in praise, which saw the presence, blessing, favour and deliverance of the Lord. But when they were disobedient in worship this same blessing and favour lifted and rather than deliverance, they experienced defeat. The Lord wanted His people to walk in blessing, but it was dependent upon their **COMPLETE OBEDIENCE**.

When we praise, the Lord's presence descends, and our spirit realigns as our praise causes us to magnify the Lord over the issues and strongholds of life. As we praise, He is magnified, and it is this magnification through our obedience which diminishes the walls of the Jericho's in our lives. As we have already touched on, the truth of the matter is that strongholds are areas in our lives that consumer our time, focus and our strength. When we bring a sacrifice of praise though we are taking the same time, focus and strength and redirecting to where it belongs, the Lord. As we turn to Him, we stop magnifying the issue and start magnifying the Lord who is above the issue. It is this spiritual re-alignment that causes us to feel the breakthrough. Within us this generates a fresh sense of hope and strength within our inner man. Whilst this is the blessing of obedience in worship, the problem can be that the feeling that praise generates can end up being the thing that we seek for in praise. We miss the point of praise and focus in on what it does for us. Because praise makes us feel better about the things of life, we can end up being more focused on praising to feel good than praising in obedience. Praise can almost become a self-seeking act, where we start declaring the truths of the Lord that we might start feeling better about our circumstances. Praise becomes more about us than it does about God. That is not praise, that is satisfying the flesh! Any time we are looking at what we get out of praise our focus is askew.

We don't praise for breakthrough. When we praise, we declare the truth of who God is and what He has done without concern for whether he will or won't deal with the strongholds that lay before us. Our motivation in praise can never be to give in order to get. That makes it transactional rather than sacrificial.

Obedience unto the word of the Lord led the Israelites to praise which was to lead to worship. If all we do is focus on praise, then we are falling short of complete obedience. Whilst the blessing of the Lord descended on the people of Israel as they praised at Jericho, it quickly lifted when their praise did not lead to worship! Praise is part of our worship, but not all of it. If we want to walk in the continual blessing of the Lord, our praise should always lead us to worship! It is the path of obedience that sees us walk in the blessing of the Lord.

When we overemphasis praise, through a misunderstanding of what it does for us, like Achan we rob God of the worship He deserves. We need to understand that praise has absolutely nothing to do with us. 'Us' should never ever be a factor in praise. What we feel when praising and what we get out of it feeling wise is irrelevant. Praise in terms of an individual is all about re-establishing the Lord as the main point of focus in our lives. It is about declaring the truths of God so that our faith in Him becomes greater than our faith in the issues of life. Faith comes by hearing, and hearing by the word of God (Rom 10:17).

Praise is all about Him! Any time we enter the picture it is a warning sign that the flesh is looking to be satisfied.

As believers we need to understand that praise is a part of our worship, but it is not the entirety of it. Whenever a truth of scripture is taken to an extreme, we end up in error. That is the danger of an overemphasis on praise. As we have seen in the points above, when praise is overemphasised, it is usually because a misunderstanding of what it is, what it does for God and/or what it does for us. All of these aspects reveal that these errors have a root of flesh within them, which means that our worship is not in spirit. We are called not to be a people of praise, but a people who sacrificially praise the Lord as part of our worship.

A Focus on Hype

In terms of worship, hype can be defined as a way man looks to create a certain atmosphere through extravagant or intense proclamations and sounds.

Worship can sometimes be looked at as a way to get people's attention and get them involved. Songs are chosen by their loudness, beat and the appeal of their sound. There is an encouragement for the people to be loud. The music is looked at as the means to engage the audience, with the focus being on the performance from up the front. Such seeks to create an atmosphere of hype that draws people into the spectacle of what's happening. Whilst the motives may seem pure, all that we are actually achieving is creating an atmosphere of false praise. When the focus is on hype, the focus is on the flesh.

Hype can be likened to excessive positivity where the MC or worship leader vocally attempts to stir and raise a reaction from the audience. Secular artists do the same thing at concerts as a means of gaining audience participation and generating a positive atmosphere. Hype in worship attempts to do the exact same thing just in a Christian setting.

Hype can be seen as the focus when the agenda of praise and worship is to rouse the audience. Terms like 'we have to be contemporary', 'we have to appeal to the young people', 'we need to keep the congregation engaged' are all rooted in appealing to the flesh in worship. The priority of worship is never the congregation. Such stems from a lack of proper teaching and understanding in regard to praise and worship.

If our purpose in worship is to create an atmosphere that will attract and keep an audience, then we have missed the mark. Such hype will be somewhat successful in terms of achieving its goal, but it is never meeting the mark in terms of true worship. It is worship based in the flesh seeking to appeal to the flesh.

Our Worship varies based on our feelings

A great indicator on a personnel level that the flesh is evident in our worship is when our worship is based on our feelings. When we are feeling good, our worship is off the charts, fully committed, hands raised and voice loud. When we are not feeling so good though, our worship is reserved and muted. And when we are somewhere in between so is our worship.

If this is the case, what it reveals is that our flesh is actually dictating the worship that we give. We are letting our flesh tells us what we are going to sacrifice in worship. When we are good, we sacrifice a lot, but when we are down, we don't have much to sacrifice. Rather than dying to the flesh in worship, we are allowing flesh to determine our worship.

The reality of life is that on any given day we may be feeling up, down or in between. That though should never determine our worship. As we have seen in this section, worship is sacrificial by definition. That means dying to the flesh rather than letting it determine our worship. Our worship should be constant. Our flesh may be up and down, but our worship should always be up.

Our Worship varies based on the songs

As individuals we all have certain music preferences, likes and dislikes. This though should not impact on our worship. Our preference for styles of worship or periods of worship should not come into it. If our worship rises and falls based on the song, then it may be an indicator that we are looking for our flesh to be satisfied in worship.

One of the greatest banes of a worship leaders' life would be the barrage of recommendations they get in regard to songs that "I Like". When what we like determines our level of worship, we are satisfying the flesh more than we are worshipping in spirit. If we are worshipping in spirit, then as long as the songs align with the Word of God, we should be able to worship. That should in fact be the only thing that matters. Our worship should never be dictated to by what satisfies our ears.

Our Worship avoids any periods of quietness

In our look at the worship of the sinful woman who anointed the feet of Jesus we noted that worship is not dependent upon music or singing. In the modern era though our flesh has become so used to the aid of music and singing in our giving of worship that we have forgotten how to worship in silence and in the quiet place where we wait upon and hear the still small voice of the Lord (1 Kings 19:11-12). We have lost that intimate touch with the Spirit and in so doing have become awkward in the silence because we don't know what to do. The flesh doesn't like it and resists it because it feels wrong. We have rise and fall in songs, we go from soft to loud, engaging the flesh, but all we really do is yo-yo our way through. We avoid the still place because our flesh is not engaged when the external noise dies down.

When we are on a first date with someone any silence feels awkward, so we desperately try to keep the conversation going at all costs. In a long-term marriage though, a couple can comfortably be together for hours without ever saying a word. There is no awkwardness in the silence, just peace. The difference exists because of the intimacy of the relationship.

So too is it with our worship. When we have that intimacy with the Spirit, the silence doesn't feel awkward, it feels natural. It is a place where we are comfortable, resting in the presence of the Lord. If we don't have this experience or peace though it is an indicator that the flesh may be present in our worship. The flesh will always feel uncomfortable in the quietness of His presence!

Summary

In this section we have looked at several indicators that can reveal to us that the flesh may be involved in our worship. This is by no means an extensive list, but more of a guide to help us as believers identify within ourselves if our worship needs refining. As believers and congregations, in order to offer the true worship that is required of us, we have to make sure that our worship is in spirit and not in flesh. In all simplicity, the key to identifying any flesh in worship is to look for the satisfaction of self or the focus on 'I'. 'I like that song', 'I got a lot out of that worship', 'I found this easy to worship to' and so on and so forth. All highlight a focus on self in worship, which shows that the flesh is present.

To be truly able to worship in spirit all elements of the flesh have to be removed. It is a continual struggle and one that we as believers cannot afford to be lax in. It is a daily practice to make sure that we are holy and acceptable as living sacrifices. There is a standard of worship that we as believers are called to, and we have a responsibility to make sure that we fulfill it.

We are to be worshippers who worship in spirit.

Reflection

Provided below are some questions for the Individual, the Worship team and for the Church to consider. These have been provided as a means to help us to reflect on that which we have considered in this section. These questions are meant to be introspective and as such a perceived negative answer in this section is not necessarily a bad thing. What it shows is that we are honestly looking at our worship with a heart to change in those areas where it is required. An open honest introspection shows that we have the heart to be true worshippers.

Before reading over the below questions would you pray with me:

> *Lord, as I read over these questions, I pray that you would soften my heart and allow me to hear the prompting of your Holy Spirit through them.*
>
> *Holy Spirit, would you lead and guide me and please reveal to me any areas in my worship where the flesh may be present. Would you help me to deal with these areas and die to those things that have hindered my worship.*
>
> *Lord, would you help me to be one who denies the flesh, takes up their cross and presents themselves as a living sacrifice. Lord, help me to be one who worships you in spirit.*
>
> *In Jesus name,*
>
> *Amen.*

REFLECTION

For the Individual

- What is my motivation in worship?

- Do I look to get something out of worship?

- How do I judge a good worship service?

- Do I worship more to songs that I like?

- Does the type of worship dictate my participation in worship?

- Do I come to Church ready to worship? Have I prepared?

- Am I self-conscious in worship?

- Do I want to be noticed in worship?

For the Worship Team

- Where is my value derived?

- Do I seek affirmation for my performance?

- Do I worship the same in the congregation as I do up the front?

- Would I be offended if I was rested from being up the front?

- Am I worshipping by example or for example?

- What kind of songs do we sing? Why?

- Is the lyricality of our songs focused more on the individual than God?

For the Church

- What is the purpose of our worship?

- Is our worship focused on attracting people?

- Do we look to create an appealing environment for worship?

- What is the focus of the songs we sing?

- Do we have an overemphasis on praise?

- Does our praise lead the congregation into worship?

- Do we do any teaching on worship?

- Do we worship in spirit with a focus on the Spirit?

In Error

Or

In Truth

In Error Or In Truth

*We are of God. He who knows God hears us; he who is not of God does not hear us. By this we know the **spirit of truth** and the **spirit of error**. (1Jn 4:6) NKJV*

Test all things; hold fast what is good. (1Th 5:21) NKJV

We now turn our attention to looking at worship in error as opposed to worship in truth. The danger that exists for believers, as stated in our previous section, is that although we may be worshipping the Lord, if we are doing it in error rather than truth, then we are falling short of the standard of true worship that the Father is seeking.

Just as we observed in our previous section that there is a battle between the flesh and spirit, so too is there a battle between error and truth in worship. Truth doesn't change, truth is always truth! Whether everyone believes it, or just a few, it is still truth. In its battle against truth though, error seeks to undermine and dilute truth through continual attack. Whereas the signs of the flesh are generally more obvious in its conflict with the Spirit, the hallmarks of error can be extremely subtle and hard to spot. Error initially is very small and generally not that far removed from truth which is what makes it so effective. Error doesn't try and deny the truth; it seeks to corrupt the truth by introducing deception. Error always starts as a minor deviation. Error is like a small chip in a windscreen, which may at first seem inconspicuous or not worth dealing with, but if undealt with it will spread and have disastrous results. A little leaven will work through the batch! Whilst error may start small, it can quickly grow and when it does it quickly increases the distance between itself and truth.

It is for this reason that one of the constant warnings of the New Testament writers was for New Testament believers to be on guard against error. Their appeal was for believers to constantly be on watch and make sure that they knew the truth and were clinging to it. The New Testament writers understood the dangers of error and the impacts it could have on the people of God if it was not detected and promptly dealt with. Lets look at some of these passages which highlight the battle of truth against error in the Church and the people of God.:

2 PETER 3:3.

> *that you may be mindful of* **the words which were spoken before** *by the holy prophets, and of the commandment of us, the apostles of the Lord and Savior, knowing this first: that* **scoffers will come** *in the last days, walking according to their own lusts, (2Pe 3:2-3) NKJV*

In this epistle, Peter was writing to believers and seeking to bring their minds back to the truths of the prophets and the commandments that the apostles had spoken. Given the Church was so fresh here we may be tempted to ask why was it necessary for Peter to write and warn the New Testament Church of scoffers? Even though the Church was still relatively young, they had to have these truths in remembrance and be on guard, for there was going to come scoffers who would seek to introduce error into their beliefs.

The Greek word for scoffer as used here is only used twice in the New Testament and carries the meaning of "a derider, by implication a false teacher". Peter's warning to believers was not to be mindful of those without that would laugh and mock at our faith. The appeal of Peter was for believers to understand the truths of scripture as taught by the prophets and apostles because there was going to come from **WITHIN** the Church false teachers seeking to draw believers away from the truth with deceitful teaching. It would be teaching that aligned with who these false teachers wanted God to be and teaching that allowed them to satisfy their own lusts. It would be teaching that was erroneous and would take believers from the path of truth if they weren't careful.

Peters' plea was for believers to know the truth so that they would not be deceived by false teaching and allow error into their lives.

MATTHEW 18:7.

> *Woe to the world because of **offenses**! For **offenses** must come, but woe to that man by whom the **offense** comes! (Mat 18:7) NKJV*

Within this verse the word offence is used three times and in each instance it is the same Greek word, 'skandalon'. This word means "a trap stick or a snare" and is translated "occasion to fall, offence, thing that offends or stumbling block". It carries with it the thought of an impediment that inhibits the walk of an individual, whether they are caught by the snare and unable to move, or whether they trip as they walk.

Jesus was stating that there were things that were going to come that would inhibit the walk of believers. There would be things designed to ensnare us and to cause our walk in faith to be hindered. There would be things that were intended to pull us from the truth of the Word to a place of error. The thing about stumbling blocks and traps is that they are not immediately obvious. That is actually part of their design. If they were obvious, they would be of no effect. They are deliberately designed to be concealed, hidden and not able to be detected until after they have had their desired effect.

Whilst Jesus started by saying woe to the world, He closed by stating "woe to the man by whom the offence comes". These stumbling blocks, snares, stick traps would come through individuals. Individuals would lay these traps to ensnare others.

1 TIMOTHY 4:1-6.

> *Now the Spirit expressly says that in latter times some will* **depart** *from the faith,* ***giving heed*** *to deceiving spirits and doctrines of demons, (1Ti 4:1) NKJV*

Paul in writing to his son in the faith, Timothy, admonished him that in the latter times some would depart from the faith. Again, what we see clearly defined here is that Paul was talking about believers. He was talking to those who had believed and followed the truth. These same believers though would withdraw and step away from the truth that they had once followed. Why? Because they would give heed to seducing spirits and doctrines of demons. This is strong language by Paul, but what does it mean? Let's look at the keywords from this sentence.

Giving heed: - to *hold* the mind *towards*, that is, *pay attention to, be cautious about, apply oneself to, adhere to.*

Deceiving: *roving* (as a *tramp*), that is, (by implication) an *impostor* or *misleader.*

Doctrine of Demons: instruction, learning, teaching, doctrine of devils.

If we put this all together, what we see is that believers depart from the truth when they pay attention to the teaching and doctrine of misleading and deceiving spirits that are in fact impostors! Rather than giving heed to the truth that they have been instructed in, they stray to the path of error, being misled and end up in doctrine that is contrary to the Word of God. In other words, they end up in error!

In a lot of cases this is no doubt not a deliberate action, but rather one that occurs because the truth is not constantly re-referred to.

1 JOHN 4:1-6.

Similarly to Paul, the apostle John likewise gave his audience an admonition to be on guard and try the spirits:

> *Beloved, do not believe every spirit, but **test the spirits**, whether they are of God; because many **false prophets** have gone out into the world. (1Jn 4:1) NKJV*

In this verse John said that we are not to believe every spirit but rather test them. The reason we need to do this is because there is a Spirit that comes from God, but there is also a spirit which comes through false prophets. These two are not the same and in order to correctly identify them we need to test them. There is a true Spirit and there is a false spirit.

As we progress in this chapter of 1 John, we see this terminology expanded upon. In verse 2 and 3 John we read of the Spirit of God and the Spirit of antichrist. Again, we see John contrast that which is right with that which is false, truth versus error.

Then in verse 6, John sums things up by saying:

> *We are of God. He who knows God hears us; he who is not of God does not hear us. By this we know the **spirit of truth** and the **spirit of error**. (1Jn 4:6) NKJV*

There is a spirit of truth and there is a spirit of error. The two stand opposed to each other. That which comes through the false prophets, through antichrist is a spirit of error that seeks to draw people from the truth.

The Greek word for error as used in this verse means "to objectively fraudulence, subjectively to stray from orthodoxy or piety". Fraudulence is something that has the appearance of truth but is in fact something that is greatly inferior and its whole purpose is to take advantage of its victims. Fraud aims to deceive its victims by pretending to be something it's not. Error pretends to be truth, but it isn't. Error occurs when we are deceived by a lie and wander from the path of truth.

In this passage, whilst comparing the same two things, John used a number of different titles to reference them. He referred to these two spirits as:

Spirit of God		Spirit of False Prophets
Spirit of God	V's	Spirit of Antichrist
Spirit of Truth		Spirit of Error

Truth and Error are opposites. The Spirit of God is truth, but the spirit of error seeks to draw us away from truth by imitating it. As believers our safeguard is to know truth and hold to it!

1 CORINTHIANS 2:12-14.

> *Now we have received, not the **spirit of the world**, but **the Spirit who is from God**, that we might know the things that have been freely given to us by God. These things we also speak, not in words which man's wisdom teaches but which the Holy Spirit teaches, comparing spiritual things with spiritual. (1Co 2:12-13) NKJV*

In this verse Paul highlights to us that there is the spirit of God and the spirit of the world. The spirit of the world is error! As believers we have received not the spirit of the world, but the spirit of God.

Paul then goes on to say that we have received the spirit of God that we might know the things that God has freely given to us. In other words, the Spirit of God, the spirit of truth reveals truth to us. The spirit of truth brings illumination and understanding of truth. We have received His spirit of truth that we might grow in our understanding of truth.

Paul then concludes by stating that he spoke the truths that God had revealed to him through the Spirit of truth. He did not speak according to the spirit of the world, which is man's wisdom, but spoke according to that which the Holy Spirit taught. Paul here contrasts man's wisdom with the Holy Spirits teaching. The spirit of the world produces teaching that seems like wisdom in the eyes of man. It has an appearance of truth, but it is not. The only truth is that which the Spirit of Truth brings!

Paul then gave us a check that we are to apply; we are to compare spiritual things with spiritual. We always check spiritual things against the Spirit of truth. The Spirit of truth is our measuring stick and our error detector. The Spirit of truth will always either confirm spiritual things as truth or reveal the error in them, but we have to take the time to seek Him about these.

JUDE 1-4.

> *Beloved, while I was very diligent to write to you concerning our common salvation, I found it necessary to write to you exhorting* **you to contend earnestly for the faith** *which was once for all delivered to the saints. For certain men have crept in unnoticed, who long ago were marked out for this condemnation, ungodly men,* **who turn the grace of our God into lewdness** *and deny the only Lord God and our Lord Jesus Christ. (Jud 1:3-4) NKJV*

Jude began his epistle by informing his readers that he had desired to write to them regarding their salvation. He felt he couldn't do this though because he saw the need to write to them and call them to contend for the faith that they had received. The word used by Jude for contend here means "to struggle for, to earnestly contend for." Jude's call was not for the believers to just recall what they had once believed, he was urging them to earnestly contend for the truth that they had once received. His call was for them to hold to that which they had received.

Again we have an early church situation and may wonder why would Jude feel the need to urge them to do this? The reason for this is given in verse 4; certain men had crept into the fellowship, under the radar of those who were there, and were twisting the truths of God. Strong's translates the Greek word crept to mean: "to settle in alongside, that is, lodge stealthily". These were believers, but their beliefs and doctrines contained error. Jude's could see the error in their teachings, and his imploration was for the other Church members to remember the foundational truths they had been taught so that they too would also be able to clearly see the error that was seeking to work its way through the Church.

Jesus warns of a similar thing in Matthew 7:

> *"Beware of* **false prophets, who come to you in sheep's clothing**, *but inwardly they are ravenous wolves. (Mat 7:15) NKJV*

In Jude these individuals had the appearance of fellow brethren and had settled into the Church. They were however turning the grace of God to fulfill their own wanton lusts and agenda's. They took the truth of God and through deception were twisting it. That is why Jude had the urgency to write what he did. He saw the greater need for the truth to be contended for so that believers would be spared from error. If truth is not contended and fought for it will be eroded and lost. Just as Paul implored, we are to look beyond the surface and compare spiritual things with the Spirit of truth.

Truth is like a house. In order for it to be kept and maintained, there is continual work that must be done. If this work isn't attended to, the house becomes run down and over time it will start to fall apart. So too must truth be maintained (or contended for). If not, error will erode truth to a point where it is unrecognisable and a shell of what it once represented. Error is always seeking to erode truth!

GALATIANS 3:1.

> *O foolish Galatians!* **Who has bewitched you that you should not obey the truth**, *before whose eyes Jesus Christ was clearly portrayed among you as crucified? (Gal 3:1) NKJV*

Paul in the above verse questioned the Galatians believers as to who had bewitched them to stop obeying the truth. The Galatians had been following the truth but for some reason had stopped. The Greek word for bewitched according to Strong's means: "to *malign*, that is, (by extension) to *fascinate* (by false representations)".

The Galatians had been led from the path of truth by false representations. A false representation is something that pretends to be one thing but actually is another. It is a con, a trick. The Galatians had been presented with truth that wasn't truth and had been deceived into error. Having been bewitched they had left the path of truth.

Error always looks like truth and that is what makes it so effective. As believers our greatest guard is to always be referring back to and reminding ourselves of truth so that we are ready to defend ourselves against error.

Through the above examples, we see that Jesus and the New Testament writers constantly warned and admonished New Testament believers regarding the need to hold fast to the truth. The New Testament Church had a constant battle of error attacking truth.

There is the Spirit of truth and the spirit of error. Error always stands in opposition to truth. As the above verses highlight, error is always seeking to come against the foundations of truth that we as believers hold to. Error is always looking to find its way in through a crack. It just wants a starting point and if it can find that, it will seek to grow and force itself into other areas, gradually causing the crack to become a great canyon. Its mission is to cause us to stray from the path of truth.

As believers in the modern Church, we need to be aware that the exact same battle still exists today. As believers we not only need to know the truth but continually contend for it and constantly look to the truth of the Word to make sure that we have not strayed into error.

The enemy always attacks truth with lies in an effort to dilute and erode it. He doesn't deny the truth, he twists it. He presents something that resembles the truth, but is actually a lie. It is a trap, a snare, a stumbling block, designed to cause a hindrance in our walk. It is when we act upon the lie, that we stumble from the way of truth that we end up in the way of error.

Error in Action

Having looked at how truth and error stand in opposition to each other and the need for us to beware of error, we will now turn out attention to looking at just how error comes into existence in our lives and Churches.

To do this we will turn back to the example of Adam and Eve that we looked at earlier on in this text. For our purposes here we will work through Genesis 3:1-7 verse by verse in order to fully see what it reveals to us.

GENESIS 3:1.

> *Now the serpent was more cunning than any beast of the field which the LORD God had made. And he said to the woman,* **"Has God indeed said**, *'You shall not eat* **of every tree** *of the garden'?" (Gen 3:1)* NKJV

Genesis tells us that the serpent came and asked Eve a question. Whilst this is an interaction we are no doubt familiar with, it is an interaction that should prompt a few questions in our mind. Firstly, why did the serpent come and question Eve and not Adam? In Genesis chapter 2 we read that the Lord spoke to Adam regarding not eating from the tree of knowledge of good and evil. This was a communication between God and Adam alone. It is not until after this encounter that we then read that God then created the woman. Eve was not around when God spoke to Adam! In other words, Adam heard the command directly from God, but Eve heard the command directly from her husband. It was a message that had been relayed. The reason the serpent questioned Eve and not Adam was because Eve's understanding was based on what Adam told her and as such there was a greater chance for a misunderstanding to have occurred.

A second question for us to consider is why did the serpent question Eve on what God had said? He didn't ask Eve why she couldn't eat of the tree; his question was specific to what God had actually said! "Has God said?" Or in other words, what were God's specific words on this topic? Satan questioned Eve to check what her level of understanding of God's command was. The Bible tells us that God's Word is truth (John 17:17). The enemy will always seek to test our comprehension and understanding of the truth, God's Word, to see if there is a weakness in our understanding that he can exploit with deception. Note his question, "Did God say you shall not eat of **EVERY TREE**?" God had never said this and the enemy knew that. God had only spoken about not eating from **ONE** tree not **EVERY** tree! Satan here sought to engage the woman in conversation and through that conversation test her knowledge of the truth to see if there was a point of weakness.

The enemy will always question our understanding of the Word of God, to try and find a weakness. If we recall the temptation of Jesus when He was in the wilderness for forty days, the second time that Satan tempted Jesus, he challenged Him as to His understanding of the Word (Matt 4:6-7).

> *And said to Him, "If You are the Son of God, throw Yourself down.* **For it is written***: He shall give His angels charge over you,' and, In their hands they shall bear you up, lest you dash your foot against a stone.' " (Mat 4:6) NKJV*

In this passage Satan quoted directly from Psalm 91:11-12. He presented this passage to Jesus, albeit out of context, in order to test Jesus' understanding of the Word just like he did with Eve. Jesus was the Word made flesh. His understanding was perfect for He was the living, walking embodiment of the Word. There was no weakness in His understanding. For us as believers though we need to make sure that we are ever growing in our understanding of the truth of the Word. We have to always maintain a teachable spirit that allows the Holy Spirit to guide us into a greater understanding of the truth of the Word for it is the truth that protects us from error. If the enemy can see a weakness in our understanding of the truth, he will attempt exploit it.

GENESIS 3:2-3.

> *And the woman said to the serpent, "We may eat the fruit of the trees of the garden; but of the fruit of the tree which is in the midst*

> *of the garden, God has said, 'You shall not eat it, nor shall you touch it, lest you die.' " (Gen 3:2-3) NKJV*

Note the response of Eve! Upon first reading it seems like she has answered the serpent well. But if we stop and examine it a little further, what we see is that her response was **PARTIALLY** correct. Eve confirmed that it was only one tree that God told them not to eat from, but she also added something that God did not say. If we jump back to Genesis 2, we can read exactly what the Lord had originally said to Adam regarding the tree.

> *And the LORD God commanded the man, saying, "Of every tree of the garden you may freely eat; but of the tree of the knowledge of good and evil* **you shall not eat, for in the day that you eat of it you shall surely die."** *(Gen 2:16-17) NKJV*

Note that the Lord never said anything about not touching the fruit! The Lord told Adam not to eat the fruit. There was nothing mentioned about touching the fruit. Somewhere between the interaction between the Lord and Adam and the Woman and the serpent, the original command or Words of God had changed and been expanded. How this came to be we are not told. We cannot say for certain if this was just Eve adding to the command, or if this actually occurred through Adam's communication with his wife in regard to the commands of the Lord. It is possible that in relaying the command of the Lord to his wife, Adam added to it in an effort to try and communicate the seriousness of God's word. What it does highlight though is the absolute necessity of knowing the truth of God and holding fast to it.

What we see here is that the Word of the Lord was added to by man. Whilst God's original command had not changed, man had changed his own understanding of it by adding to it. Whilst possibly done with good intentions, this actually diluted the power of the truth and it is this dilution that provided the enemy with an 'in'. Eve's understanding of the truth was lacking, which provided a door for the enemy to enter with deceit.

GENESIS 3:4-5.

> *Then the serpent said to the woman, "You will not surely die. For God knows that in the day you eat of it your eyes will be opened, and you will be like God, knowing good and evil." (Gen 3:4-5) NKJV*

Having tested the woman and heard her response, the serpent saw an opportunity to introduce deception. How did he deceive? He twisted the Word of God. The serpent told Eve that she wouldn't die, but that her and Adam's eyes would be opened, and they would be wise as gods. The danger of this statement of the serpent is that it contains **PARTIAL** truth.

- Adam and Eve wouldn't die when they touched the fruit.
- Adam and Eve wouldn't immediately die physically when they ate the fruit.
- Their eyes would be opened.
- They would know good and evil

What we see here is twisted truth. It is deceit that contains enough truth to make it believable. It seems right, but anything contrary to His truth is always error!

GENESIS 3:6.

> *So when the woman saw that the tree was good for food, that it was pleasant to the eyes, and a tree desirable to make one wise, **she took** of its fruit **and ate**. She also gave to her husband with her, and he ate. (Gen 3:6) NKJV*

We see here that it was a lack of understanding of the truth that allowed Adam and Eve to err. Adam and Eve had added to God's Word by stating that if they touched the fruit they would die, but God had never said this! They were never going to die from touching the fruit, death came through consumption! Bu what is the first thing that would have happened before Eve ate the fruit? She would have picked the fruit or in other words Eve would have touched it! Because Eve had added to the God's Word though, when she picked the fruit and nothing happened, i.e. she didn't die, suddenly the truth of God's Word seemed untrue. I touched it and I didn't die, nothing happened so therefore it must be fine to eat like the serpent said! Eve's lack of understanding of the truth automatically gave credence to the lie of Satan! This is the danger of not having clarity around the truth of God. Misunderstanding opens the door for deceit from which error follows.

Eve took of the fruit, and she ate, sharing it with her husband. Adam and Eve were deceived by the serpent and left the path of truth to the path of error. Adam and Eve ended up in error because they had been deceived by the lie of the serpent.

It is interesting to compare 1 John 2:16 with the account of Eve's transgression.

> *For all that is in the world—the lust of the flesh, the lust of the eyes, and the pride of life—is not of the Father but is of the world. (1Jn 2:16) NKJV*

John summed up the things of the world as the lust of the flesh, the lust of the eyes and the pride of life. When we apply the truths of this to the account we read in Genesis 3:6 we see:

The lust of the flesh – Eve saw the tree was good **for food**.

The lust of the eyes – it was **pleasant to the eyes**.

The pride of life – and a tree to be desired to **make one wise**.

We see in Genesis the same three things spoken of by John. It is the spirit of the world that seeks to deceive individuals and cause them to err from the truth! If we look further in scripture, we see that the three exact same things were also employed by Satan against Jesus in an effort to cause Him to err as shown below:

1 JOHN 2:16	EVE GENESIS 3:6	JESUS TEMPTATION MATT 4
The lust of the **flesh**	The tree was good for *food*	Command these stones to be *bread* vs 3
The lust of the **eyes**	The tree was ***pleasant to the eyes***	I will give you all the world kingdoms ***you see*** vs 8-9
The **Pride** of Life	*A tree to be **desired to make one wise.***	Cast yourself off the ***temple if you are the Son of God*** vs 6 (i.e. Prove yourself.)

The spirit of the world wars against the truth in an effort to lead us into error. It came against Eve, it came against Jesus, and it comes against believers today. Its deceit will always contain partial truth. Thats what makes it believable and palatable, but it will only ever end in error. Our only defence is to know the truth, the Word of God. Eve had a wrong understanding of the truth and because of this engaged the deceit presented to her which led to error. Jesus though never engaged, he simply quoted scripture in response. No conversation, just rebuttal each time. "It is written". He knew the truth and wasn't led away by the spirit of the world.

GENESIS 3:7.

> *Then the eyes of both of them were opened, and they knew that they were naked; and they sewed fig leaves together and made themselves coverings. (Gen 3:7) NKJV*

After eating of the fruit of the tree of the knowledge of good and evil the eyes of Adam and Eve were opened. But what exactly where their eyes opened to? Their eyes were opened to the truth! Once their eyes were opened, the veil of deceit was lifted and they could see the truth. They saw Gods truth and they also saw that they had erred from it.

A similar thing is seen in the life of the apostle Paul. Paul was initially an enemy of the Church, persecuting it and any believers that he came across. Paul was under the deception that he was living a Godly life and following the truth of God's word. Then he had the Damascus Road experience where the Lord appeared to him, and he lost his sight for a short period. The Lord then sent Ananias to him who prayed that the Lord would open his eyes. From the moment that his eyes opened, the veil of deception was removed, and Saul saw the truth which resulted in his life being completely transformed.

As believers we need to pray that our eyes would be opened to the truth. This is the appeal of the Lord to the Church of Laodicea in Revelation 3:17. The Laodicean Church was under a cloud of deceit and saw themselves in a way that the Lord didn't. The Lord counselled them to let Him anoint their eyes with salve that they might see correctly. They needed their eyes opened to the truth. As believers and Churches, we need to seek the Lord in the same way. We need to ask Him to open our eyes that we may see the truth clearly.

The enemy disrupts our vision with deceit. When our vision isn't clear we end up in error. This is what we see with Adam and Eve. When the Lord opens our eyes though we see the truth and we see it clearly. Clear vision of the truth prevents us from ending up in error!

We see with Adam and Eve that the enemy was able to cause them to stray from the truth by introducing a lie which caused them to err. They ended up in error because they were deceived and didn't hold to the truth of the Word. The lies of the enemy seek to cause man to stumble from the path of truth and end up in error. He seeks to deceive us through the spirit of the world and blur our vision. It is a truth seen throughout the Bible and a tactic that the enemy continues to use today. Error occurs when we stray from truth.

Summary

So far in this section we have considered truth and error in terms of our overall walk with the Lord. This understanding is vital in our Christian walks, but as we move forward here, we will focus in specifically on how truth and error affect our worship. We as believers need to understand the application that truth and error have in regard to our worship. There is truth and there is also error. We need to be aware of both! Whilst we may think that error will be obvious, it can creep into our worship subtly and gradually and cause us to stray from and miss the standard of true. The spirit of the world will seek to pull us from God's truth and into deceit that is based in partial truth.

We are called to be a people who worship the Lord in spirit and in truth. There is a Godly standard that we have been called to. It is a path that we must strive for. Every believer has a unique journey and at points we may like Eve have believed a lie, or we may have inherited the error through the teaching of others. Ours though is to seek the truth and be the kind of worshippers that the Father is looking for! For us to become that, we need to make sure that there is no error in what we offer. It is my prayer and hope that the following pages help you somewhat in that journey.

You may not necessarily agree with everything that is presented in the following pages, but I would encourage you to take the time to seek the Lord and ask Him to open your eyes to the truth of His Word before moving forward. That is not to say that you should just adopt everything presented, that would not be wise. But neither would it be wise to immediately dismiss everything just because we don't agree with one or two points. What I would encourage is for you to be open to what God wants to speak to you through the pages that follow. As Paul said we are to compare spiritual things with spiritual (1 Cor 2:12-13) and my encouragement would be to take that which you read and prayerfully compare it with the Word and seek His truth. It is His Spirit of Truth that will lead us into truth and protect us from error.

Worship in Error

My people are destroyed for lack of knowledge. Because you have rejected knowledge, I also will reject you from being priest for Me; Because you have forgotten the law of your God, I also will forget your children. (Hos 4:6) NKJV

Worship in error may seem like a topic of little or little to no relevance to New Testament believers and Churches. But it is important to remember that we are not talking about false worship here. False worship and worship in error are two completely different things as previously discussed. False worship is done by those that follow false gods. It is worship that is completely false with no focus on the one true God. Worship in error though, is worship offered by New Testament believers and Churches unto the one true God. We are talking about worship given by New Testament believers unto the Lord. It is worship, but it is worship in error, and it exists in both individuals and Churches alike. It is vital that as believers we understand that our worship has the potential to contain error.

Throughout this study our purpose is to examine how we as believers fulfill the standard of true worship. As a reminder, the Words of Jesus were that those who worship the Lord must worship in spirit and in truth. It is His standard! The responsibility lies with us to meet it.

As we have seen in our previous section, there are always forces at work seeking to pull us from the path of true worship. The lies of the enemy will always seek to divert us from the path of truth and cause us to walk in the path of error. Worship in error can be unintentional, and it can be unknown to the ones offering it. In fact, I would go as far to say that in most cases worship in error is undeliberate and generally stems from a place of good intentions. It is not a choice to worship in error, it happens because we are unaware of the fact that we have strayed from truth. As Hosea says in the verse quoted above, it stems from a lack of knowledge. Knowledge of the truth is the greatest protection that we have from error.

Worship in error occurs when we unwittingly or unknowingly have believed a lie and as a result have been deceived to stray from the truth of God's Word. It can be something that we have adopted, or it may be the way that we have been brought up. It is not false worship, but nor does it meet the standard of true that the Lord is seeking. It is worship offered by believers, but it is worship in error.

But how does this happen in worship? How can those that believe and follow the Lord worship in error? Such sounds like a contradiction! Let's take some time to look at some Biblical examples that highlight worship that has strayed from the path of truth and resulted in error and see what we can glean. As we will see, this is worship offered by those who follow the Lord. It has all the appearances of being right, but it isn't. It is worship of the Lord, but it is worship in error.

Nadab and Abihu

In the book of Leviticus, shortly after the consecration of Aaron and his sons to the offices of High Priest and Priests, we read of the account Nadab and Abihu. Nadab and Abihu were the two elder sons of Aaron and served as Aaronic priests in the Tabernacle of Moses. They served under their father, having been chosen by the Lord to this office.

Earlier in the book of Exodus the Lord had laid out for Aaron and His sons the duties and functioning of the Tabernacle of Moses. When we get to Exodus 30 we read of the commands that the Lord gave specifically surrounding the Golden Altar of incense and the ministry that was to occur there. The Lord gave very specific commands of **how** ministry was to occur at this altar and **when** this ministry was to occur. The Lord even went as far as to say that no "strange incense" should be offered upon this altar.

> ***You shall not offer strange incense on it,*** *or a burnt offering, or a grain offering; nor shall you pour a drink offering on it. (Exo 30:9) NKJV*

The Lord was very clear and very deliberate in explaining what was acceptable and what wasn't acceptable for the worship that was to be offered at the Golden Altar.

When we come to Leviticus 10 though, we read:

> *Then Nadab and Abihu, the sons of Aaron, each took his censer and put fire in it, put incense on it, and offered* ***profane(strange) fire*** *before the* LORD, **which He had not commanded them**. *So fire went out from the LORD and devoured them, and they died before the LORD. (Lev 10:1-2)*

Contrary to the explicit command of the Lord, Nadab and Abihu offered strange or profane fire. The word for strange used here is the exact same word as used in Exodus 30 regarding the strange incense the Lord told them not to offer. The exact nature of what this error was we are not sure and expositors have different views about just what it may have been. They may have offered non-holy fire, or they may have approached the altar at a time that the Lord had not commanded. What we do know for sure though is that their error centred around Nadab and Abihu not following the commands of the Lord. The strange fire that they offered was not in line with what the Lord had spoken and revealed regarding the operation of the Tabernacle.

Nadab and Abihu offered something that the Lord had not commanded them to. They deviated from His truth and were found in error. They had believed a lie that what they were doing was right and would be accepted by the Lord. It wasn't! It was worship in error and fell short of God's divine standard.

It is important for us to remember here that these were the sons of Aaron, they were of the family of the High Priest. They were serving in the Tabernacle of Moses, and this service was a part of their approach unto the Lord. These were literally the leaders of the Church in the wilderness, and they were in the act of worship. They would have been dressed in their priestly robes, and they would have been using the implements of the Tabernacle that were usually prescribed for this type of worship. Everything about this worship would have looked authentic. From a strictly visual perspective, this ticked all of the boxes. It looked right, it smelled right, and it seemed right. This though was worship in error. They came before the Lord to worship, but they did not meet His standard of true. Nadab and Abihu were worshipping the Lord, yet not according to His standard. They had erred from the path of truth.

Possibly the most alarming thing about this account is how quickly error crept in. The Tabernacle and the priests had only just been consecrated to the Lord. His fire had only just fallen in acceptance of the sacrifices presented. Despite all this, we see error in the worship of Nadab and Abihu. They were seeking to worship the Lord, but they were not worshipping in truth. Error crept into their worship almost instantaneously.

King David

King David is seen in the Word as a worshipper of the Lord, so it might seem strange to look at an icon of the Bible who is generally associated as a standard of worship to follow. But as we will see, David at times worshipped in error. Whilst David was one who worshipped in spirit as we saw in the previous section, the example we will consider here highlights that there was an instance when his worship was also in error. It was worship in spirit and in error!

The example we will consider is contained in 2 Samuel 6:1-10 and 1 Chronicles 13:1-14 when David looked to bring the Ark of the Lord up to the city of Jerusalem. I would encourage you to read over these two accounts before moving forward here.

During the time of Eli the priest, when the prophet Samuel was still young, the Ark of the Lord had been taken down to a battle between Israel and the Philistines. It was brought down as a means to rally the troops of Israel and bring about victory for the nation. Victory did not occur though! Israel was defeated by their enemies and the Ark was captured by the Philistine army. Whilst the Philistines initially held on to the Ark, the judgement of the Lord broke out against them and after passing it from village to village as a means of dealing with the problem, they soon returned it to the nation of Israel. The Ark was returned to Beth Shemesh and then made its way to Kiriath Jearim, to the house of Abinadab. There the Ark of the Lord stayed, through the reign of Saul and up to the point when David felt impressed to bring it up to Jerusalem.

David's desire to bring the Ark of the Lord to Jerusalem was not just an impulse but rather something that he contemplated and considered. Whilst David had the initial desire to do this, he then consulted with his leaders, his captains of thousands, his captains of hundreds and indeed the congregation of Israel about what he wanted to do. This was something that David gave thought to and sought advice on. His error did not come from rushing into something without thinking. Everyone he consulted responded in agreement that this was a good thing to do and indeed it was. In all truthfulness it was something that should have happened long ago!

David gathered all Israel together: people, priests, soldiers and leaders. All went together to Kiriath Jearim to bring the Ark of the Lord up to Jerusalem. In order to transport the Ark across the distance, they picked up the Ark and placed it upon a new cart. They didn't use an old cart, but a new one which had not been used for anything else. This cart was driven by Uzza and Ahio who were the sons of Abinadab, the man whose house the Ark had been at, and is likely that they served in the same office of priests that we read of with their brother Eleazer in 1 Samuel 7:1. As the Uzzah and Ahio drove the cart towards Jerusalem, David and all Israel worshipped before the Lord:

> *Then David and all Israel **played music before God** with all their might, with **singing**, on **harps**, on **stringed instruments**, on **tambourines**, on **cymbals**, and with **trumpets**. (1Ch 13:8) NKJV*

This was a joyous time, where the people worshipped before the Lord with everything they had. It was a time of jubilant celebration with music and singing. It would have been quite the worship service! As the Ark travelled passed the threshing floor of Nachon, the oxen stumbled and caused the Ark to become unsteady and move upon the cart. In an effort to steady the Ark of the Lord, Uzzah put out his hand and placed it upon the Ark to secure it. Whilst his intentions may have been good, the actions of Uzzah aroused the anger of the Lord:

> *Then the anger of the LORD was aroused against Uzza, and He struck him because he put his hand to the ark; and he died there before God. (1Ch 13:10) NKJV*

David, possibly like us reading this passage, was taken back by the actions of the Lord. The journey of the Ark was ceased as David was too afraid to bring the Ark into his city and the Ark of the Lord was left at the house of Obed-Edom. What had started as such a joyous time of celebration before the Lord ended in sombreness under the Judgement of the Lord. What a stark contrast exists in this small passage of scripture.

As we consider this, our questions are possibly similar to those that went through David's mind.

- How could the judgement of the Lord break out when the people were worshipping God with all their might?
- How could Uzzah be struck down for protecting the Ark?
- Why would the Lord do this?

To understand the fulness of what happened here, we need to take some time to consider just what the Ark of the Lord was and why God did this.

THE ARK OF THE LORD.

The Ark of the Lord is first introduced to us in the book of Exodus when the Lord gave unto Moses the revelation of the Tabernacle of Moses (Ex 25). The Ark was essentially a large box with a lid. It was made of shittim wood and overlaid with pure gold inside and out. On both sides of the Ark were two golden rings, into which would fit the golden poles which were used for transporting the Ark. Upon the top of the box structure of the Ark was a border which was also known as a crown, which extended around the top perimeter of the Ark. On top of this sat the lid known as the mercy seat. The lid itself was made entirely of gold and was an incredible piece of craftsmanship. The lid was made from one piece of gold, yet it was fashioned in such a way that from it two golden cherubim rose, one on the left and one on the right. These two cherubim looked towards each other and down with a focus on the gap between them. They looked down at an angle to the top of the mercy seat.

Under the lid of the Ark resided the two tables of stone inscribed with the ten commandments of the Lord, the golden jar of manna that had been collected as a memorial for the nation of Israel and Aarons rod that had budded (Heb 9).

The Ark was the holiest of all pieces of tabernacle furniture and the only piece of furniture to reside in the Most Holy Place. The High Priest would minister to the Ark only once a year on the great Day of Atonement. On this day the High Priest would take the blood of the atonement sacrifice and anoint the lid of the Ark, between the Cherubim with the atonement blood.

The Ark was the throne of God upon the earth. It was on top of the blood-stained mercy seat that the presence of the Lord resided within the Tabernacle of Moses. It was here that Moses would go and commune with the Lord face to face. It was here that the presence would go out to lead Israel and it was here that the presence returned.

The Ark is synonymous with the presence of God. It was where He dwelt in the nation of Israel. It was from where He communicated. It was His throne. It was Most Holy.

Having briefly considered the Ark, we can move on to consider our next question.

WHY GOD DID THIS.

Having learned that the Ark represented the presence of God on the earth we now turn our attention to understand the reasons why the Lord's judgement broke out against Uzzah. To do this we must turn back to the book of Numbers.

When the Lord gave to Israel the plans for the Tabernacle of Moses and all its furniture, Israel was in the midst of what would be forty years of wilderness wanderings. They were in a sense a nomadic people and as such everything had to be frequently transported. Because of this the Lord gave to the Levites, those responsible for the task of packing, moving and resetting up the Tabernacle of Moses, provisions to undertake this role.

In Numbers 7:1-9 we read that when the Tabernacle had been set up, anointed and consecrated that the leaders of the tribes of Israel made an offering unto the Lord of six covered carts and twelve oxen. The Lord then spoke to Moses in regard to these and told him to give them unto the Levites for their service in the Tabernacle. The Levites had the responsibility for the transport of the tabernacle. Every time that the cloud lifted, and the Israelites moved in the wilderness, the Levites had to pack up the Tabernacle and transport it to the new spot where they would re-set it up. The carts would be of great assistance in this service.

As we continue in Numbers 7 we read:

> *So Moses took the carts and the oxen, and gave them to the Levites.* **Two carts and four oxen he gave to the sons of Gershon,** *according to their service;* **and four carts and eight oxen he gave to the sons of Merari,** *according to*

their service, under the authority of Ithamar the son of Aaron the priest. **But to the sons of Kohath he gave none,** *because theirs was the service of the holy things,* **which they carried on their shoulders.** *(Num 7:6-9) NKJV*

From above we learn that the sons of Gershon were given two carts, the sons of Merari were given four carts, but the sons of Kohath were given no carts. Kohath received no carts because their service required them to bear their items upon their shoulders. Everything that those of the clan of Kohath were responsible for was to be carried.

One of the items that the sons of Kohath were responsible for was the Ark of the Lord (Num 4). Throughout all the wanderings of Israel in the wilderness and into the promised land, the Ark was carried on the shoulders of the priests. Their service was to carry. Kohath were given no carts for the things they were responsible for. Throughout the journeyings of Israel the Ark was never borne on a cart by the people of Israel until we come to David. David was the first Israelite to have the Ark placed on a cart! Based on that we then have to ask, if the Ark was never intended to be transported on a cart, why would David do this? Why would David have the Ark transported on not just a cart, but a new cart? Where did this thought come from that was contrary to the truth of the Word of God?

We find our answer to this question in 1 Samuel 6 when the Ark of the Lord was in the territory of the Philistines. After suffering under the judgements of the Lord, the Philistines had had enough of the Ark and wanted to return it to the nation of Israel. They wanted to do it in a way though that would make sure the Lord's judgement would lift from them, so they called for their priests and diviners for how this should be undertaken. Part of the advice that was given was:

> *Now therefore,* **make a new cart***, take two milk cows which have never been yoked, and hitch the cows to the cart; and take their calves home, away from them.* **Then take the ark of the LORD and set it on the cart;** *and put the articles of gold which you are returning to Him as a trespass offering in a*

> *chest by its side. Then send it away, and let it go. (1Sa 6:7-8)*
> NKJV

The only times in scripture that the Ark of the Lord was transported upon not just a cart, but a new cart, is when the Philistines returned it to Israel and when David sought to bring it to Jerusalem. At no other time in scripture did the Ark of the Lord ever travel on a cart, old or new! The error that David made was that he looked to the example of the world for how to handle the presence of the Lord. David looked to his frame of reference. David looked to what the world had done, and he didn't just copy and adapt what the Philistines had done, he replicated them exactly! He built a new cart and had the Ark transported upon it. He failed to ever look at the Word of God and simply copied what he had heard. His worship was in error.

The reason that the judgement of the Lord broke out was because the presence of the Lord was being mishandled by a people who should have known better! Israel were God's people, and they should have known the requirements surrounding the Ark. God had made it very clear to them how His Ark was to be transported. Rather than seek out His truth though, they copied the example of the world. What the Philistines did looked successful, let's just do that! By looking to the example of the world, they ended up in error.

David and the people of Israel were worshipping the Lord. Their focus was upon Him solely as they played music and sang. This was a literal mobile worship service! Again, from an outside perspective none would doubt that this was worship of the Lord. People were giving of all their might in worship unto the Lord. Yet it was not worship in truth. It was worship in error! David's error was that he believed the lie that the people of God could look to the world for how to handle the presence of the Lord. David's error occurred because **HE NEVER CHECKED THE TRUTH,** he just assumed his approach was correct! It is a stark warning for us to be mindful of.

Blessing and Judgement

In both of the examples of Nahab and Abihu and king David, we see the truth of the verse we opened this section with, "for lack of knowledge my people perish." In both cases worship in error led to the judgement of the Lord in the lives of those who offered it.

I am not suggesting that as New Testament believers we walk under the same possibility if our worship is in error. It is important that we understand that we are under a different dispensation, the dispensation of grace and not law, where we experience the mercy and long suffering of God. God is indeed gracious to His people.

What I would say though, is that if we are worshipping in error, then as the above examples reveal, we are not going to be walking in the fulness of the blessing of the Lord. Whilst, as we have discussed already, we do not worship for a blessing, there is however a blessing that flows when the people of God worship in truth. Any time there is error in our worship, we rob ourselves of this. Obedience commands a blessing (Deu 28:1-2, 11:27, Luke 11:28), and God can never **FULLY** bless that which doesn't align **FULLY** with His Word.

Nadab and Abihu were worshipping before the Lord. There were at the newly erected Tabernacle of Moses, in their priestly robes operating in what looked like priestly service, but the Lord couldn't bless them because their worship was not in line with the truth He had revealed. David and all Israel were worshipping before the Lord and seeking to honour the Lord with the Ark. It would have been an incredible sight to see this travelling procession of praise and worship, but the Lord couldn't bless them either because their worship was in error. He endured it for a moment, but He couldn't bless it.

So too is it with us as New Testament believers and Churches! God cannot fully bless that which doesn't fully align with His Word. God cannot bless that which is in error. God is looking for worshippers that worship in truth. He is seeking for such. Such should serve as a prompt for us as New Testament believers to examine our own worship. If king David, the man after God's own heart, could unknowingly wander into error in his worship then so to may we.

Just because worship has the appearance of being right in the eyes of man, doesn't mean that it necessarily meets the standard of true. Nadab, Abihu and King David are clear examples of this. We may well say but God looks on the heart, but to say or imply that intention supersedes or overrules obedience is false and unbiblical. For the people of God, ignorance of the truth does not justify disobedience to it. We cannot stand upon the grounds of "I didn't know". Obedience commands a blessing, and the opposite is also true. God cannot bless something that is not rooted in obedience! To do so would be to dilute the importance of the truth. It is why God's actions against Uzzah seem so extreme. He had to highlight to David the enormity of the error in his approach. If He had simply blessed David's approach, the error would have only grown!

If we, as the people of God, are to experience the fulness of the blessing of the Lord upon our worship, then we need to make sure that there is no error in it. We have to approach the Lord according to His truth, and not ours!

Summary

Hopefully through this section we have been able to highlight how worship in error occurs and that as believers and followers of God, our worship is still open to error. The appearance of our worship may be right. Our intentions may be pure. Error however can still be there. Such is not written to inspire fear, but rather to encourage openness within us to be able to hear the truth that the Spirit would wish to speak to His people and His Church.

Having seen the issue of error in Godly worship, the question now becomes how do we avoid this and worship in truth? This leads us to our next section.

Worship in Truth

Call unto me, and I will answer thee, and shew thee great and mighty things, which thou knowest not. (Jer 33:3)

We now turn our focus to the topic of worship in truth and consider how we as believers can fulfill this standard that the Lord has set. In this section we will endeavour to answer the questions of what does it mean to worship in truth and how do we as believers do that?

Before we can consider how we are to worship in truth and what it looks like, we need to understand from a biblical perspective what truth is. What is truth? In John chapter 17 we read of an account where Jesus was praying unto his Father. As Jesus' prayer continued, the focus of His prayer turned to His disciples:

Sanctify them by Your truth. **Your word is truth***. (Joh 17:17) NKJV*

In this short and succinct verse, we have our definition of truth. The Word of the Lord is truth! The Word is what the Lord spoke by the Spirit through the various writers of the scripture and gave to mankind as the Bible, the Word of God. The Bible is the truth of God. It is truth and within it the Lord has communicated everything to man that man needs to know! The Word of the Father is truth. The following verses further testify to this truth:

> ***The words of the LORD are pure*** *words: as silver tried in a furnace of earth, purified seven times. (Psa 12:6) KJV*

> ***The law of the LORD is perfect****, converting the soul:* ***the testimony of the LORD is sure****, making wise the simple.* ***The statutes of the LORD are right****, rejoicing the heart:* ***the commandment of the LORD is pure****, enlightening the eyes. (Psa 19:7-8) KJV*

> *You are near, O LORD,* ***And all Your commandments are truth****. Concerning Your testimonies, I have known of old that You have founded them forever. (Psa 119:151-152) NKJV*

> *In Him you also trusted,* ***after you heard the word of truth, the gospel of your salvation;*** *in whom also, having believed, you were sealed with the Holy Spirit of promise, (Eph 1:13) NKJV*

The sixty-six books of the Bible which make up the one book are the truth of God to and for man. His Word is truth.

From this discovery we can glean that for our worship to be in truth, it has to be according to the Word of God for that is truth. His Word lays out for us how we are to worship in truth. God has set forth how He is to be approached by man and if we are to worship in truth we must follow His directions.

To worship in truth is to worship in accordance with the Word of God. There is a divine order that God has given unto man in regard to worship. Within the Word of God, the Lord has explained to man how He is to be approached. He has outlined the way of truth for us, but there is a responsibility upon us as believers to look at His truth and make sure that our worship is in line with this. It is the responsibility of man to make sure he not only knows the truth but that his worship also aligns with it.

Let us now turn to an example from scripture that highlights this to us.

Again with the Ark

Just as we did with our look at worship in error, in looking at worship in truth we will look at the life of king David. The example we will consider here looks at the second time that king David sought to bring the Ark of the Lord up to Jerusalem, picking up just after the passage that we looked at with worship in error. After initially ceasing in his efforts to bring the Ark of the Lord to Jerusalem because of the results of error, David decided to make one more attempt to bring the Ark up. This account is detailed for us in 2 Samuel 6:12-16 and 1 Chronicles 15:1-29. I would again encourage you to read over these portions of scripture before moving forward.

In the months that the Ark of the Lord remained at the house of Obed-Edom, Obed-Edom was greatly blessed by the Lord. This blessing was reported to David, and my thoughts are that this must have stirred Davids thinking, as his heart changed from not wanting anything to do with the Ark to again desiring to bring the Ark up into the city of Jerusalem into the tent he had prepared for it. The report concerning the blessing of Obed Edom caused a shift in king David. This time though, things would be different. David had the benefit of time to reflect on what had happened and to seek the Lord about it.

As David prepared to bring the Ark of the Lord up, he summoned the children of Aaron and the Levites, the priests of Israel unto himself. Note the address of David in speaking to the Priests:

> *And David called for Zadok and Abiathar the priests, and for the Levites: for Uriel, Asaiah, Joel, Shemaiah, Eliel, and Amminadab. He said to them, "You are the heads of the fathers' houses of the Levites; sanctify yourselves, you and your brethren,* **that you may bring up the ark of the LORD God of Israel** *to the place I have prepared for it. For because you did not do it the first time, the LORD our God broke out against us, because* **we did not consult Him about the proper order***." (1Ch 15:11-13) NKJV*

Note the words of David in verse 13. "Because you did not do it at first, the Lord made a breach upon us, for we did not seek Him about the **PROPER ORDER"**. Where did this new understanding come from for David? What brought about the realisation that they had not followed the proper order? How did David even know that there was a proper order?

No doubt that after experiencing the judgement of the Lord in his first attempt of bringing up the Ark and then hearing about how the house of Obed Edom was blessed because of the Ark of the Lord, David went to the Lord with questions. Why is he being blessed, yet I experienced your judgement? Why is there a difference between his experience and mine?

In this time between the attempts at bringing up the Ark David no doubt sought the Lord and subsequently had a light bulb moment as the Lord illuminated His truth unto David. I believe that the Lord enabled David to realise that the reason that the judgement of the Lord had broken out was because he had not done things correctly. David had a realisation that the Lord had a proper order for how He was to be approached. In bringing up the Ark of the Lord the first time, David had not sought the Lord on how this was to be done, he had just assumed how to do it, and he assumed wrongly. He had not sought the Lord about His proper order. He had sought the people about bringing the Ark up to Jerusalem, but he didn't seek the Lord.

So where did David discover this proper order of the Lord? Where did he go to find it so that his second attempt to bring up the Ark, would not end the same way as his first? As we continue reading in Chronicles we discover where David found this proper order.

> *So the priests and the Levites sanctified themselves to bring up the ark of the LORD God of Israel. And the children of* ***the Levites bore the ark of God on their shoulders****, by its poles, as* ***Moses had commanded according to the word of the LORD****. (1Ch 15:14-15) NKJV*

David found the due order in the Word of the Lord. As David looked into the Word of the Lord, the Lord highlighted the very things that we discovered in our look at worship in error. David would have read of who was responsible for the Ark and how it was to be transported. David read over the Word of the Lord and as he did, the Lord unveiled His truth to him. He discovered how it was recorded for the Ark that bore the presence of the Lord to be handled. It is the same light bulb scenario that so many of us believers have experienced. How did I miss that? How did I not see that before? As we look intently into His Word, we discover His truth. This was true for David, and it is true for all believers. It is within His Word that we discover His truth.

As David discovered the truth of the Lord, his worship changed. Note how the Ark was transported in this instance. Rather than again trying to transport the Ark of the Lord on a new cart, this time the Ark was carried upon the shoulders of the Levites. David's approach completely changed. He had learned God's truth! The staves or poles of the Ark were gathered, they were placed in the rings on the side of the Ark and the Ark was carried according to the Word of the Lord. The throne of God upon the earth was carried upon the shoulders of His priests according to the Word of the Lord. How different was David's approach this time around! David went from copying the world to following the truth of the Lord.

It was only when David turned to the Word of the Lord that he found the **PROPER ORDER** that God had outlined and was able to worship in truth. It was as David took the time to look at his worship in the light of the Word of truth, that he saw the error of his ways. What had initially seemed so right, was now clearly seen as error. This error was only visibly though because David compared it to truth. Error always seems right until it is compared to truth! What must have gone through David's heart when he had this realisation? David after all was a man after God's own heart. How remorseful he must have been for his error! How he must have repented of his anger towards the Lord (1 Chr 13:11). How disappointed must he have been in his own actions?

It was the truth of the Word of the Lord that showed David his error. It had all been written down and given to Moses. It had been recorded for Israel to refer to. The truth was there. The Priests and Levites should have known it. King David should have known it (Deut 17:14-20). The truth was always there, and it was always available. God hadn't hidden it; man just hadn't availed himself of it! God had given man His truth and there was a responsibility upon man to worship according to it.

Because David sought out the truth of the Lord in regard to how to worship, we see that David's second approach had a much different outcome than his first. Rather than the judgement of the Lord we read of the blessing of the Lord upon David in this endeavour. The Ark was brought up to Jerusalem and it was placed in the tent that David had pitched for it.

> *So they brought the ark of God, and set it in the midst of the tabernacle that David had erected for it. Then they offered burnt offerings and peace offerings before God. (1Ch 16:1) NKJV*

This tent became known as the Tabernacle of David and was a place of worship for all Israel. Whilst the Tabernacle of Moses was still in operation, the Lord used this Tabernacle of David to communicate further truth to mankind in regard to worship!

Following the Ark being placed in this tent David offered burnt offering and peace offerings. He then blessed the people in the name of the Lord and sent everyone home with a gift. It was a time of joy and celebration and stood in stark contrast to how David's effort had ended in his first attempt at bringing the Ark up. Blessing flowed as David and all Israel worshipped in truth! The difference in the two approaches was determined through David's obedience to the truth. Blessing followed David's obedience to the truth.

If we compare what occurred in David's first and second approach with the Ark, we discover three key differences that surrounded David's handling of the Ark.

SANCTIFICATION.

> *So the priests and the Levites **sanctified** themselves to bring up the ark of the LORD God of Israel. (1Ch 15:14). KJV*

To be sanctified is to be set apart, to be made clean, to be made holy. The priests and the Levites took the time to sanctify themselves before handling the Ark of the Lord. This was no doubt truth that David had learned from looking into the Word of God.

In David's first instance of bringing up the Ark we do not read of this happening. We read of no preparation of the priests before they came near the presence of God. In fact, it wasn't even Levitical priest who drove the cart! In the first instance we read of presumption. David presumed in his handling of the presence of God.

In the second instance though we see preparation. The priests prepared before they came near and handled that which represented the presence of the Lord. They took the time to prepare themselves in accordance with the Word of the Lord. In the second instance there was no casualness in handling the presence of the Lord.

Between the first and the second attempt we see presumption and casualness compared to preparation and reverence.

SACRIFICE.

> *And so it was, when God helped the Levites who bore the ark of the covenant of the LORD, that they offered seven bulls and seven rams. (1Ch 15:26) NKJV*

> *And so it was, when those bearing the ark of the LORD had gone six paces, that he sacrificed oxen and fatted sheep. (2Sa 6:13) NKJV*

Whilst the Chronicles passage would suggest that there was one sacrifice made when it was seen that the judgement of the Lord didn't break out upon the Levites when they lifted the Ark, some expositors believe that the passage from Samuel could suggest that upon every seventh step of the priests, a sacrifice was made. In other words, throughout the journey of the Ark to Mt. Zion, sacrifice was continually being offered unto the Lord upon every seventh step of the priests bearing the Ark. Such may sound excessive but if we compare it to the sacrifices offered at the dedication of Solomons temple it actually sounds like a valid conclusion. (2 Chron 7:5)

Whilst we do not know for sure, what we can surmise is that when David brought the Ark up the second time he did so with sacrifice. In the bringing up of the Ark of the Lord the first time there was no sacrifice. There was no shedding of blood. There was singing, dancing and worship but there was no sacrifice. This changed on the second occasion when David discerned that there was a proper order. The truth of scripture is that there can be no approaching the presence of the Lord without the blood of sacrifice. There is a linkage between the two that is evident from Genesis to Revelation. It is a truth that was clearly put forth in the Tabernacle of Moses and it is clearly a truth that David learned as he sought out the proper order of the Lord.

The Word of the Lord showed David the necessity of sacrifice surrounding His presence.

HANDLING OF THE ARK.

> *And the children of the Levites bore the ark of God **on their shoulders**, by its poles, as Moses had commanded according to the word of the LORD. (1Ch 15:15)*

As we have already touched on, by far the biggest contrast between Davids first and second attempt of bringing the Ark of the Lord up into Jerusalem is with how the Ark was handled. Rather than the Ark being driven on a new cart by two appointed priests, here the Ark of the Lord was born upon the shoulders of those that the Lord had appointed to transport it.

On the second attempt, David had the children of Levi bear the Ark of the Lord upon their shoulders according to the Word of the Lord. Just as the Ark had been carried throughout its wilderness wanderings, so it was carried here. David had discovered the truth! As he looked in the Word of the Lord, he discovered that the Ark was never meant to be transported on a cart, it was meant to be carried.

How clearer things must have become for David when he read this. How his perception of what happened in his first attempt must have changed. How repentant he must have been!

David was not too proud to admit that he had erred. He had missed the mark initially but having discovered the truth he made sure to correct his course and follow the proper order. God's presence can only ever be handled in accordance with His Word. If we do that, blessing will follow.

The differences and similarities in comparing the two efforts of David to bring the Ark to Jerusalem can be seen in the table below. What should immediately stick out is the vastness of the similarities between the two approaches. As we look over these, we can see that the two approaches, in terms of the actions of God's people, have a lot of points in common! Such should be a warning to every believer. We have to dive deeper than appearances with worship. We must always measure our approach against the truth of the Word of the Lord.

FIRST ATTEMPT WITH THE ARK	SECOND ATTEMPT WITH THE ARK
All Israel gathered	*All Israel gathered*
Priests Gathered	*Priests Gathered*
Levites Gathered	*Levites Gathered*
	Priests Sanctified
Presumption	*Preparation*
Worship with all their might	*Worship with all their might*
Singing	*Singing*
Instruments	*Instruments*
	Sacrifice
Ark on a Cart	***Ark carried by the priests***
Following the worlds way	*Following Gods way*
Judgement	*Blessing*
Worship in Error	**Worship in Truth**

It is only when we look at these two attempts in the light of the truth of the Word that we can clearly see that one was in error, and one was in truth. It is the truth of the Word that shows us the error of our ways. It was only as David looked into the Word of God that he learned the proper order and was able to worship in truth.

Hopefully from a look at the above we can see that the Lord has laid out within His Word a due order for how man is to approach Him in worship. It is a truth laid out from Genesis through to Revelation. But like David, if we are to be a people who worship in truth, we must look at our own worship in the light of His glorious Word. His Word is truth and if we are to worship in truth, it has to be according to His Word.

The purpose of this section is not do a full exposition of worship, but rather to highlight to us from the life of David how we as New Testament believers' worship in truth. God's roadmap for us to be able to worship in truth is contained with His Word. It is all there. The danger for believers exists when we rely on our presumptions of knowing how the Lord is to be approached. This was a trap that David fell into. David was a man after God's own heart, yet even he had to learn that for worship to meet the Lord's standards it must be performed not just in spirit but also according to the truth of His Word.

The verse that we opened this section with tells us that if we call to the Lord, He will tell us great and unsearchable things. David had a lack of knowledge in how to approach the Lord because he didn't call and seek the Lord for how to do it. He presumed and operated in ignorance. David though learned from his mistakes! He called and sought the Lord, and the Lord revealed to him things that he didn't know. The Lord revealed the truth of how He was to be approached to David.

The same invitation exists for us. The promise of the Lord is that if we call, He will answer. The way that we solve the error of a lack of knowledge is to seek the Lord for His truth. There is a responsibility upon the people of God to seek the Lord and make sure that the worship that we offer aligns with the truth of God's Word. We cannot afford to operate in presumption and tradition. We must look to the truth of the Word and make sure that our worship aligns.

Summary

For us as New Testament believers to be able to meet the standard of true worship, we need to make sure that the worship that we offer aligns completely with the Word of God. The example that we considered with David in this section shows us just how similar worship in error and worship in truth can appear. We may be convinced that what we are doing is correct, but if we allow the light of the truth of the Word to shine upon it, we may find that there are things that are missing or out of place. This was David's experience, and it would be a position of pride for us to presume that we could never make that same mistake. As humans we are all fallible and apt at falling into tradition. Our responsibility though is to worship in truth and not just a portion of truth but to worship wholly in truth. As believers we ever need to check the alignment of our worship with the Word of God. May we ever be a people who call to the Lord and seek Him for His truth. If we call, He will answer!

Identifying Error in our Worship

We will now consider some points that can help us to identify worship that may be in error in our lives and in our Churches. In our look at king David, as we considered his first and second attempts at bringing up the Ark of the Lord, we saw that it is not our heart attitude that determines whether our worship is in truth, but rather the alignment of our worship with the truth of the Word of the Lord.

The same influence that came against David is one that is still prevalent with believers and Churches today. David's worship was drawn into error because he was influenced by the world, as he looked to the example of the Philistines in regard to how to handle the presence of the Lord. While most of us as New Testament believers would instantly recoil at that suggestion, we must be aware that the enemy is always seeking to pull our worship from the standard of true. He doesn't do this with a bulldozer, but slowly and subtly by gently trying to influence us with the spirit of the world and leading us to the path of error. As we saw at the start of this the spirit of the world stands opposed to the Spirit of God (1 Cor 2:12-14, 1 Jhn 2:16), and where the Spirit of God seeks to lead us into truth, the spirit of the world is focused on drawing us away from truth and subtly leading us into error.

For believers and Churches, we need to be aware of the subtleties with which the spirit of the world seeks to capture our attention and subsequently affect our worship. It is a gradual influence but one that eventually takes over (1 Cor 5:6, Gal 5:9). We will refer to this as the Lot Paradigm. and will spend some time briefly exploring this thought before then going on to look at some possible areas of error within our worship.

The Lot Paradigm

We are first introduced to Lot in Genesis 11 where we learn that he was the nephew of Abraham. It would appear from scripture that Lots parents had passed away and Abraham, his uncle, had taken over as his custodian. When the Lord called Abraham to the land of promise, Lot journeyed with his uncle out from Haran. After his great faith journey, Abraham would eventually settle in the land of Canaan, and it was there that he and Lot would for the first time separate. The possessions of the two men had become so great that the land could not support them staying together. It is at this point that we see the life of Lot take a turn. It is a turn that may initially seem innocuous, but as we will soon see, this turn led to a journey for Lot that would affect the rest of his life in a devastating way. This journey was in fact a series of successive choices by Lot, but as we will see each of these choices led Lot further and further under the influence of the spirit of the world. Let's see what we can learn from Lot's journey:

LOT LOOKED TOWARD SODOM.

After having lived and journeyed together for so long, Abraham had the realisation that so great were the possessions and flocks of he and Lot that the land could not support them both. The herdsmen of both men were starting to fight and there were now quarrels where there had always been peace. Abraham was not willing for strife to come between he and his nephews relationship, so he spoke to Lot and said:

> *Is not the whole land before you? Please separate from me. If you take the left, then I will go to the right; or, if you go to the right, then I will go to the left." (Gen 13:9)* NKJV

Whilst Abraham was the senior person and had every right to make the first choice, he deferred to his nephew and graciously let him have first choice. Lot surveyed the land around him, and he saw the plain of Jordan, in which was the city of Sodom.

> ***And Lot lifted his eyes and saw*** *all the plain of Jordan, that it was well watered everywhere (before the LORD destroyed Sodom and Gomorrah) like the garden of the LORD, like the land of Egypt as you go toward Zoar. (Gen 13:10) NKJV*

Lot saw that this land was well watered and would be great for flocks, but there is more to it than just that. In the plains were towns and cities. There was civilisation. Lot had left Haran with his uncle and journeyed with him somewhat nomadically. When a famine came upon the land they went down to Egypt and dwelt there. Lot had experienced the cities of the world and rather than live the nomadic life of His uncle, Lot was drawn to the system of the world.

As Abraham gave his nephew the choice, Lot looked, he saw the world and he was drawn to it.

LOOKED PITCHED HIS TENT TOWARD SODOM.

After choosing the plains, Lot separated from his uncle and departed.

> *Then Lot chose for himself all the plain of Jordan, and Lot journeyed east. And they separated from each other. Abram dwelt in the land of Canaan, and Lot dwelt in the cities of the plain and pitched his tent even as far as Sodom. (Gen 13:11-12)*

Abraham dwelt in the land of Canaan, but Lot dwelled in the cities of the plain. Lot had looked down and seen that the plains of the Jordan would be good for his flocks, but he also saw the cities and towns of the region and how that they would be good for him. Lot didn't have to live in the city, but he chose too! Lot could have been out in the plains with his flocks and herds, but he chose not to be. Lot chose to enter the world.

Now as yet Lot was not living in Sodom, but notice the wording of verse 12:

> *and **pitched his tent toward** Sodom. (Gen 13:12) KJV*
>
> *and **pitched his tent even as far as** Sodom. (Gen 13:12) NKJV*

In other words, while Lot dwelt in the cities of the plain, his tent at times was pitched toward or in the region of Sodom. Now details are never accidently included in the Word of God. Whether Lot pitched his tent toward Sodom or whether he at times moved his tent to the region of Sodom, we discover the same truth. Not only did Lot to choose to live in a city, but there was an unmistakable pull of Sodom upon his life. Lot was attracted to Sodom.

But why would this be? In the next verse of Genesis 13 we are told that the men of Sodom were exceedingly wicked and sinful before the Lord (Gen 13:13). This was no doubt a reputation that was widely known, and yet despite that reputation Lot was drawn to it. Lot, who had witnessed the faith journey of his uncle and seen first-hand Abraham's relationship with the Lord. was enchanted by the world. There was something about Sodom that caught Lot's eyes and kept his attention. Now he wasn't yet living there, but his focus was clearly there. His eyes were well and truly on the world.

LOT LIVING IN SODOM.

The next time we read of Lot is in Genesis 14. There we read of a battle that took place as the kings of Shinar, Ellasar, Elam and Tidal king of nations made war against the kings of Sodom, Gomorrah, Admah, Zebolim and Bela.

The king of Sodom and his allies were defeated in this battle and were plundered by the raiding armies. In verse 12 we are told:

> ***They also took Lot,*** *Abram's brother's son **who dwelt in Sodom,** and his goods, and departed. (Gen 14:12) NKJV*

Lot was at this point now a resident of Sodom and was taken as captive by the raiding kings. Between Chapter 13 and Chapter 14 of

Genesis Lot went from being near Sodom to living in Sodom. Lot went from looking at Sodom from a distance, to pitching his tent toward and facing Sodom to now living in Sodom. There is a pull of the world that we see here with Lot, slowly but surely drawing him in.

LOT RETURNED TO SODOM.

Upon hearing of his nephew's captivity, Abraham rounded up all the men of his company and set out in pursuit. At night Abraham divided his three hundred and eighteen trained servants and attacked the raiding kings and their armies. Abraham and his servants won a great victory that day, saving Lot and returning the plunder that had been taken.

Lot had been taken from Sodom as a captive and then delivered by the uncle through Abraham's rescue effort, and yet it is evident from Genesis 18 and 19 that despite all this Lot returned again to Sodom.

Sodom had such a pull on Lot that rather than choose to stay in the safety of his uncle's protection, Lot chose to return to Sodom. Why would he go back? Why would he return to this place of trauma? The world had a pull on Lot. It had somehow entrenched itself so far within his life that he couldn't separate himself from it.

LOT WAS RELUCTANT TO LEAVE SODOM.

The next time we read of Lot is in Genesis 19 and it is a sad account indeed. At the start of Genesis 19 we are told that two angels came to Sodom to see if the reports of its depravity were correct. As they entered the town, they were meet by Lot who earnestly encouraged them to come and spend the night at his house rather than spend the night in the square. Lot clearly had an insight into what would happen to them if they stayed out in the open at night!

As we know that night the depravity of Sodom was confirmed as the men of the town surrounded Lot's house. The angels saved Lot, pulling him into the house and striking the townsmen with blindness. The angels then announced to Lot the judgement of the Lord that was coming and told him to leave Sodom. Whilst Lot does go to his son in laws to ask them to leave, he also procrastinates. He doesn't' immediately act on the warning of the angels. One would have thought that the warning of the angels would have sparked Lot into action, but it didn't. Lot was not in a hurry to leave!

At the dawn of the next day, the angels came to Lot again with a renewed urgency:

> *When the morning dawned,* **the angels urged Lot to hurry***, saying, "Arise, take your wife and your two daughters who are here, lest you be consumed in the punishment of the city." And while he lingered, the men took hold of his hand, his wife's hand, and the hands of his two daughters, the LORD being merciful to him, and they brought him out and set him outside the city. (Gen 19:15-16)*

The Angels had patiently waited for Lot through the night, but now they could wait no longer. They came and urged Lot to hurry up. There was an urgency in their action and an urgency in the need for Lot to make the decision to leave. Note though the language in verse 16:

> ***And while he lingered****, the men took hold of his hand, his wife's hand, and the hands of his two daughters, the LORD being merciful to him,* **and they brought him out and set him outside the city.** *(Gen 19:16)*

The word for lingered here according to Strong Concordance means "properly to question or hesitate, that is, (by implication) to be reluctant". Lot didn't want to leave Sodom! He had been warned of what was coming and yet there was something within him that wouldn't allow him to separate himself from the world. Such was the pull that it had upon him, that Lot hesitated to leave even though he knew staying would mean harm to him and his family. It makes no logical sense, and yet it shows how the pull of the world can infiltrate our minds and inhibit our ability for rational thoughts.

Despite his reluctance, Lot was shown mercy by the Lord as the angels literally grabbed hold of his hands and took him out of Sodom. It took the merciful interjection of the Lord for Lot to leave Sodom. It is most likely a decision he would not have been able to make on his own.

LOT WANTED A SUBSTITUTE TO SODOM.

Immediately after delivering Lot from Sodom, the angel messengers told Lot to escape for his life unto the mountains, lest he and his family be caught up in the destruction that the Lord was bringing. Lot though was not happy with this suggestion, and he responded and said:

> *Then Lot said to them, "Please, no, my lords! Indeed now, your servant has found favor in your sight, and you have increased your mercy which you have shown me by saving my life;* ***but I cannot escape to the mountains****, lest some evil overtake me and I die. See now,* ***this city is near enough to flee to****, and it is a little one; please let me escape there (is it not a little one?) and my soul shall live." (Gen 19:18-20) NKJV*

The judgement of the Lord was coming upon Sodom and its surrounding territories and despite this Lot requested to be able to go to another city rather than head to the safety of the mountains. Nothing about that makes any logical sense! Lot could not bring himself to leave the world. The world had worked its way into Lot so deeply, that he could no longer see any other reality! The world was Lot's normal, and he could not separate himself from it. Why would he not just return to Abraham?

Lot started out looking at the world, but the world became so deeply entrenched in who he was that he could not separate himself from it. When the assimilation with the world is gradual, we can be unaware of the increasing magnitude of its influence upon us because everything seems normal! The scriptures are apt when they say a little leaven leavens the whole lump! (1 Cor 5:6, Gal 5:9) Lot's life was leavened with the leaven of the world. What started with a look, ended up being all consuming.

> *Lot looked toward Sodom.*
>
> *Lot pitched his tent toward Sodom.*
>
> *Lot was living in Sodom.*
>
> *Lot returned to Sodom.*
>
> *Lot was reluctant to leave Sodom.*
>
> *Lot wanted a substitute Sodom.*

Between the first and last points above there is much that happens, but the fact of the matter is that the last point only happened because Lot looked toward the world. It starts with a look. It starts with curiosity. It may even start with seemingly good intentions, but the fact of the matter is that whenever we look to the world we start on a very dangerous path.

It would be my suggestion that the same danger that lay before Lot lays before the Church and believers in terms of worship today. There is a very real danger of the influence of the world upon the worship of believers in our times. Like David, whenever we look to the world for guidance on worship we step into the path of error.

Ours immediate response to this statement may be that we would never look to the world in regard to worship. Whilst it may seem extreme, I would go as far as to suggest that in some cases we as believers and as the New Testament Church have already gone beyond looking and have progressed beyond this to a point where we have assimilated the world into our worship. We have in fact made the same mistake as David and looked to the worlds example of how we should handle the presence of God. We have erred as Lot and assimilated the world into our spiritual lives. This assimilation with the world has gone on for so long, that its erroneous influences have become so normal in our lives and services that to speak about removing them would raise the same hesitation that Lot had in leaving Sodom. Such may seem like an incredibly strong statement, and perhaps it is, but let us take some time to consider some examples to see if there could perhaps be some truth to this.

Again, I would ask you to pray as you read over what follows and also to read over the whole section. What follows is not written to be condemnatory, but rather to provoke us in thought. At the heart of this we are endeavouring to get to the root of what true worship is and how we offer it. That is something we should all be able to agree on. In order to make sure that our worship is in truth, we have to be able to have an honest look at areas where we may have looked to the world and as a result introduced error into our worship. We need to have the same humility and openness that David had in discovering the proper order.

Lets consider some things that may highlight where we may have left the path of truth and stumbled into worship in error:

Darkness in Worship

A common theme in worship services today is to turn the lights down, or to turn them off completely, leaving the congregation in darkness during worship. The reason put forward for this is that it makes people feel more comfortable and able to worship more freely. Such sounds like a genuine reason to do so because we want individuals free and engaged in worship, but where does this thought of darkness in worship actually come from?

If we look at the Word of God, we are told:

- God is light and in Him is no darkness at all (1 Jn 1:5).
- When we come into the kingdom of God through Salvation we turn from darkness unto the light (Acts 26:18).
- In the book of Revelation, we are told that the new Jerusalem does not need a sun or a moon, for the glory of God provides all the light it needs (Rev 21:23).

Our heavenly Father, the father of lights (Jhn 1:17), sits on His throne in heaven and it is the light of the glory of His presence that illuminates it.

IDENTIFYING ERROR IN OUR WORSHIP

It is a brightness that mortal man cannot fully comprehend. It is within the brightness of this glory that the heavenly host and elders worship the Lord (Rev 4:10). Now if the worship of heaven occurs in the light, why should the worship of earth be any different?

Let's consider another example. When the Lord gave the designs to Moses for the first man made structure that would be used in regard to His worship and housing His presence, we see this same truth again exemplified. The Tabernacle of Moses had three distinct sections. The Outer Court was an open area and worship occurred here under the light of the Sun. The Holy Place and Most Holy Place though were contained within the tent of the tabernacle and covered from the light of the sun by several curtains that formed its roof. But even in these covered areas there was no darkness! The Holy Place was lit by the light of the Golden Lampstand which was attended to morning and night by the priests to ensure that there was **always** light. The Most Holy Place was lit with the light of the glory of the Lord. It would have in fact been the brightest of all the Tabernacle areas. It was here that His presence dwelt, illuminating the room.

These same truths flowed forward into the Tabernacle of David and the Temple of Solomon. At no point in any of these structures was darkness ever associated with worship. There was always light!

Whilst we have considered this very briefly, enough points should have been provided to provoke some thoughts in our minds. If the truth of the Word is that God is light and in Him is no darkness and we are to worship Him in light as Heaven and the Tabernacle systems reveal to us, then why do we create an atmosphere of darkness in our services? Why have we introduced darkness into something that has never been associated with darkness? Where does this idea come from?

If we honestly think about it, we really don't have to look to far. One only has to look to the music and the concerts of the world to see that when the music starts, the lights go off. Darkness is a consistent theme in the music performances of the world. The great error that we have made in these days is that we have looked to the example of the world. In looking at how our worship services should run, we have looked to the examples of what the world does with music to engage their audiences. We have looked to the world for how we should handle the presence of God and just like king David we have adopted their practices!

As believers and Churches, we have made the mistake of Lot. We have looked to the world and been drawn in by it. And we can probably even rationalise and justify our reasons for doing it. It has potentially been done with good intentions. The thing that we need to remember though is that error always requires justification whereas truth is always built on biblical foundation! Truth is always backed up with balanced exposition of the scriptures. Error though always requires a man-made justification that has a religious twist to make it seem plausible. Whenever we feel the need to justify something in worship it should immediately spark the question in our minds about whether what we are doing might be in error. Justification should act as an early warning alarm for us to examine what we are doing.

The Biblical truth of the matter is that darkness and worship do not belong together. True worship is done in the light. If we as the people of God cannot worship the Lord openly in the light and safety of the Church, how are we ever going to be able to live out our worship in the darkness of the world. Darkness does not allow a freedom for people to worship, all that we do when we worship in darkness is bring the world into our services. Is it at all possible that if people aren't worshipping freely in the light, that it could be because they haven't been taught about worship properly? This would be my gentle suggestion. Believers don't need a created atmosphere to worship, we need to be taught the biblical truths of worship and how to apply them!

Having considered the error of darkness, let us look at another potential error that may occur in our Churches today.

The Leading of Worship

Another area where error has crept in to worship in the Church is with how worship is led and the focus we give to it. To try and explain my thoughts around this I would like to present an example has stuck in my mind ever since I heard it. This thought is presented here for our contemplation, with some minor tweaks:

If we think of a play or a musical that is performed in front of a large audience, whilst it involves a large number of individuals performing separate and distinct functions, there are essentially three important yet distinct groups:

1. *The Performers.*

   The performers are the ones who take to the stage and undertake the actual performing of the play or the musical. These are the ones who rehearse and practice over and over to make sure that what they present is polished, refined and of a certain standard. These individuals are usually gifted in some way and have spent years honing their craft. They are confident in what they do and have the skills to back it up.

2. *The Audience.*

   These are the people in the seats. These are the ones who have come to enjoy that which is presented to them. They may not necessarily be gifted themselves, but they appreciate the gifts of the performers and the time they have spent rehearsing and practicing. These are the ones to whom the production is directed.

3. *The Prompters.*

   The prompters are an unseen part of any performance, but they play a pivotal role. The prompters are to the side, out of sight and their role is to literally prompt the performers if they forget their lines or forget to move when they should. Their role is to make sure that everything flows as smoothly as possible. They are behind the scenes yet coordinate the smooth flow of what happens.

If we were to take this example and then apply this to a Church worship environment, what we would generally say is that:

1. *The performers are the Worship team.*

   These are the ones that rehearse and practice and these are the ones who are gifted in either singing, music or both. These are the ones who are up the front on the platform or stage. They are in a place of prominence.

2. *The audience is the congregation.*

   The congregation comes to take in what the performers have rehearsed and practice. They aren't the ones "performing" but are taking in that which is being performed for them. The congregation sits or stands in the auditorium with a focus directed towards the stage and the worship team who are on it. They will join in and engage, but they are actually taking in what is coming from the front.

3. *The prompter is the Holy Spirit.*

   The Holy Spirit is the unseen one who prompts the worship leader and team on how the worship service is to flow. He is the unseen one who prompts and oversees and ensures a smooth flow.

In a lot of instances today this is the case in Church. The worship team is on the stage and the seating and lights are set up to make sure our focus is directed toward this. Sometimes the lights on the stage are brighter than those in the auditorium, just to make sure our eyes are drawn to where they should be. The focus is very much on what comes from the front.

Whilst the above may seem to resonate with us, what if this wasn't truth? What if this understanding and approach was actually error? The fact of the matter is that the understanding of worship we have outlined above is erroneous. It is not based on biblical truth but is rather an influence of the spirit of the world. The truth of worship is that it should actually look like:

1. *The performers are the Congregation.*

   Worship is in fact about the body of Christ bringing their sacrifice of worship unto the Lord. It is the congregation who are in fact the performers. They are the ones who are giving of themselves unto Him.

2. *The audience is the Lord.*

    Worship is not for people! Worship is for the Lord. As the congregation give themselves in worship they do so under the gaze of the Lord. The Lord is the one who takes in what is offered unto Him. Worship is a sacrifice that is presented to the Lord by His people.

3. *The prompter is the Worship team.*

    The role of the worship team is to assist the worship of the congregation. Their role is to prompt the congregation and ensure that the congregation is able to smoothly enter into worship. The worship team follow the leading of the Holy Spirit and prompt the congregation on where He is leading them. The role of the worship team is actually to assist the congregation with their worship, not perform it for them!

Such would seem completely contrary to how things are generally done, but it is the truth of scripture. Worship is a sacrifice that every individual has a responsibility to offer unto the Lord. It cannot be performed for them or offered on their behalf. That is not a sacrifice. Worship is about the individual giving all that they have unto their Lord and Saviour.

Worship should attract a demographic

Another common theme today is that the music, presentation and style of worship are designed to attract a target demographic. Common terminology surrounding this mode of operation is that "we want to be modern and relevant to the current generation". "We need to do what we can to reach the next generation". A common error though is that we have looked to how the world seems to impact the young people of today and we have sought to replicate it within the House of God (1 Tim 3:15). But what we see here again is the common theme of justification, "We do this because...." It is reasoning that is not based in truth!

Worship is not about being modern but nor is it about being stuck in the days of hymns or the songs of yesteryear. That is not truth either. I would actually propose that as the bride matures and grows, its worship sound, style etc should also be maturing and growing. As we grow closer into the image of Christ our worship should reflect the sound of heaven more and more.

Our worship should never be based on the needs of man, for it is not about pleasing man. Our worship should be dictated by the leading of the Spirit. Just as a preacher should wait on the Lord for the word He wants to bring, so should the music team wait on the Lord for how they are to facilitate worship so that people can present Him with their sacrifice.

If our worship is targeted to a demographic, we will attract a crowd just as any secular concert would. There are two problems with this approach though:

1. A crowd will only stay as long as they are being entertained, and as long as their needs are being met. As soon as that changes, they will leave. If our worship is led by the truth of the Spirit though, lives will be transformed.

2. There are no target demographics with God.

   For God so loved the world that He gave His only begotten Son, **_that whoever believes in Him_** *should not perish but have everlasting life. (Joh 3:16)*

   Our heavenly Father is the God of Abraham, Isaac and Jacob. He is not the Father of a generation but of **the generations**. He is the God that leaves the ninety-nine to go after the one regardless of age, gender, ethnicity etc.

The worship of God should never be focused on anything else than bringing a sacrifice unto Him. It is all about Him. We are not meant to be like the world, and we are not meant to look like the world. There should be a discernible difference.

Summary

We have highlighted here some errors in worship that potentially exist in the modern Church. We could go on to explore these in greater depths or look at things like lighting displays and smoke machines etc, but the purpose of this text is not to try and expose every potential area of error that may exist. That is not my heart and nor would I presume that I have perfect insight into all things related to worship. Far from it. The things that have been presented have been done so to prompt our thoughts. They are those things which the Lord has put on my heart in an effort to convey that we have to understand as New Testament believers and Churches that error can exist in our worship. The spirit of the world has etched itself into our services as the Church has looked unto it for thoughts and ideas surrounding the presentation of worship and music. As we have done this, the ways of the world have become so entrenched that in many cases they are standard operating procedures for many Churches. These things are so engrained that they are normal, and we don't give a second thought unto them. But if we take a step back and look at them in the light of the truth of the Word, we can see that they are in fact error.

The influence of the world is such a dangerous thing, and we need to ever take honest introspective looks at our worship to make sure that nothing has crept in. If we do not, we end up in the same situation as Lot, where we are so one with the world that we cannot see our existence without it.

Israel, the Church in the wilderness, experienced this same thing. God brought them out of Egypt with signs and wonders, displaying His superiority to the gods of Egypt, and yet Israel always still had that seed of the world in them. Constantly they longed to return to the world, because their eyes were never truly removed from it. The prophet Amos explains this when he says:

> *"Did you offer Me sacrifices and offerings In the wilderness forty years, O house of Israel? You also carried Sikkuth your king And Chiun, your idols, The star of your gods, Which you made for yourselves. (Amo 5:25-26)*

Whilst Israel was journeying through the desert, with the visible presence of God in their midst, they still clung to their idols. The leaven of the world so mixed itself through their lives, that it was indistinguishable. They worshipped God yet clung to the world. It was worship, but not true worship. Their worship was plagued by error. It's why they so quickly turned to the golden calf! The world was always there, it was never dealt with and removed.

As believers we are called to worship in truth. The greatest hindrance that we can ever have to this is by believing the deception that error could never find its way into our worship. As humans we have the same tendencies as the Israelites and as Lot. The world is always seeking to gain our attention and dilute our worship through its influence. The enemy doesn't have to stop us from worshipping; he just has to stop us worshipping in truth. The only defence against error is being open to the truth. His truth. We need to know without a doubt that what we do fully and completely aligns with the Word of God. As king David, we must look to His Word for the proper order and be prepared to change our ways where necessary.

Reflection

As we did with our section on flesh and spirit, we provide here some questions for the Individual, the Worship team and for the Church to consider. To repeat what has been said earlier, these have been provided as a means to help us take the time to reflect on that which we have read in this section. These questions are meant to be introspective and as such a perceived negative answer in this section is not necessarily a bad thing. What it shows is that we are honestly looking at our worship with a heart to change in those areas where it is required. An open honest introspection shows that we have the heart to be true worshippers.

Before reading over the questions below, would you again pray with me:

Lord as we read over these questions, we pray that you would soften our hearts and help us to allow you Spirit to reveal to us any areas that we may need to address.

Would you lead and guide us and would you reveal the truth of your Word to us. Would you please speak to us about any areas in our worship where we may have allowed the spirit of error in and been drawn away from the path of truth by the spirit of the world.

Would you help us to deal with these areas, and would you help us to be worshippers that worship you according to the truth of your Word.

Would you help us to be those who worship in truth.

In Jesus name

REFLECTION

For the Individual

- What is my understanding of worship?

- Does that align with the truth of the Word?

- What is my role in worship?

- Is my understanding based on what I have experienced?

- Is my understanding based on what I have heard?

- Is my understanding based on what I have read within the Word of the Lord?

For the Worship Team

- How do we see our role in worship?

- Are we the focus of worship or the facilitators of it?

- Do we seek the Lord for how to worship Him?

- Does the Spirit lead our worship or do our set lists determine what happens?

- Does our worship look like the world in any way?

- Are we prompting the congregation in worship or performing it for them?

For the Church

- Why do we do worship the way we do?

- Are there normal practices that are not necessarily based on truth?

- Do we teach on worship?

- Do we have external ministries teach on worship?

- Are we open to being corrected?

- Do we sense ourselves justifying the reasons for how we do worship?

- Do we take the time to reflect on if our worship still aligns with truth?

Worship In Spirit AND In Truth

It Takes Both!

> *But the hour is coming, and now is, when the true worshipers will worship the Father in spirit and truth; for the Father is seeking such to worship Him. God is Spirit, and those who worship Him must worship in spirit and truth." (Joh 4:23-24) NKJV*

Throughout this study, we considered the equation of true and in doing this we have discovered that there is worship and then there is true worship. Jesus in John 4 calls believers to be those who offer true worship, and He defines that as:

$$\underset{\text{(Right focus)}}{\text{Worship In Spirit}} + \underset{\text{(Right way)}}{\text{Worship In Truth}} = \text{True Worship}$$

As we have progressed through this study, we have looked at how we as believers and Churches can fulfill this equation by being those who worship in spirit and in truth.

They key for us to remember is that **IT TAKES BOTH!** We are called to be those who worship in spirit **AND** in truth. As a reminder:

$$\underset{\text{(Wrong Focus)}}{\substack{\text{Worship In} \\ \text{Flesh}}} + \underset{\text{(Wrong Way)}}{\substack{\text{Worship In} \\ \text{Error}}} \neq \text{True Worship}$$

IT TAKES BOTH

$$\text{Worship In Spirit} + \text{Worship In Error} \neq \text{True Worship}$$

(Right focus)   (Wrong Way)

AND

$$\text{Worship In Flesh} + \text{Worship In Truth} \neq \text{True Worship}$$

(Wrong Focus)   (Right Way)

Our worship must be in spirit and our worship must be in truth!

In seeking to try and define worship itself, we noted that the word Jesus used for worship in John 4 meant "to kiss, like a dog licking his master's hand); to fawn or crouch to, i.e. (literally or figuratively) prostrate oneself in homage (do reverence to, adore)". As we considered the implications of this, we looked at the account of the sinful woman who anointed Jesus' feet in Luke 7, and in so doing we discovered a number of aspects that form worship. We saw that:

- Worship is intentional.
- Worship requires preparation.
- Worship is positional.
- Worship is about His glory.
- Worship is based in reverence.
- Worship is sacrificial.
- Worship places and keeps Jesus at the forefront.
- Worship is done in faith.
- Worship stems from love.

- Worship is focused on Him not self.
- Worship is focused on Him not others.
- Worship is based in humility.
- Worship is not focused on time.
- Worship recognises who He is.
- Worship is transfixed on Him.
- Worship changes the atmosphere.
- Worship is not dependent on music.

Whilst this aptly describes for us the term for worship that Jesus used, in order for us to offer true worship we have to offer this type of worship in spirit and in truth. It is only when there is a harmonious balance of both spirit **AND** truth within our worship that we are offering the true worship that Jesus talks about.

In worship the Spirit provides the space to worship and the truth of the Word provides the boundaries for worship. If we just have the Word, we get focused on the boundaries and end up in a legalistic ritualistic form of worship. It becomes about adhering to the boundaries and to rules. On the other hand, if we just have the Spirit, there is infinite space and freedom that can lead us down the road of emotionalism and self-direction. It is when we have the Word and the Spirit in balance and harmony, that we have the space for the Spirit according to the truths of the Word in worship. There is a balance of Truth (Word) and Spirit.

What does it look like?

Having looked at all of this and considered the necessity for us to be a people who are true worshippers who worship in spirit and truth, the question then becomes how do we do that? What does it look like? How can we replicate it in our lives and services? The answer to all of these questions is that there is **NO** formula. There is no blueprint that we can copy and paste throughout the body of Christ. As men and women, we can tend to look for a set structure, as that is often where we can find a level of comfort in knowing what we are supposed to do. Man will often try to imitate, reproduce and recreate success. We like it when things work, and we like it when we can find ways to make it repeatable.

But that is not the case with worship. Yes, there is a standard of true worship, it must be in spirit and truth. Whilst the boundaries of the Word highlight to us an overview of what true worship is, the very fact that the Spirit is involved in our worship means that true worship is never going to be identical. The leading of the Spirit will vary from week to week, Church to Church and season to season because that is what the Spirit does. The Spirit is not always predictable (John 3:8). Whilst man looks to find systems to recreate success, God never does! God is not interested in the systems of man; He is interested in true worship. That's what He is seeking!

To try and explain things further, in the Word of God we discover that the following are all elements that are involved in true worship of the Lord. All of these elements are self-explanatory, so our comments surrounding them will be brief. What it vital for us to understand though is that these are the truths that the Word gives us about true worship. These are the boundaries truth provides:

TRUE WORSHIP INVOLVES STANDING.

> *After these things I looked, and behold, a great multitude which no one could number, of all nations, tribes, peoples, and tongues,* **standing before the throne** *and before the Lamb, clothed with white robes, with palm branches in their hands, (Rev 7:9) NKJV*

> *Praise the LORD! Praise the name of the LORD; Praise Him, O you servants of the LORD!* **You who stand in the house of the LORD***, In the courts of the house of our God, Praise the LORD, for the LORD is good; Sing praises to His name, for it is pleasant. (Psa 135:1-3) NKJV*

In natural terms when a judge walks into a courtroom those in attendance stand. When a countries national anthem is sung the people of that country stand. When a royal identity enters a room, people stand. In each of these cases people stand in honour and respect.

In terms of worship when we stand, we take that same position of honour and respect of whom we are coming before. When we stand, we actually dictate to our flesh how we will worship. It is a physical declarative act. It is not just standing; it is standing with an intended purpose.

TRUE WORSHIP INVOLVES THE PLAYING OF INSTRUMENTS.

> *Praise Him with the sound of the trumpet; Praise Him with the lute and harp! Praise Him with the timbrel and dance; Praise Him with stringed instruments and flutes! Praise Him with loud cymbals; Praise Him with clashing cymbals! (Psa 150:3-5)*
> NKJV

> *and with them Heman and Jeduthun, to sound aloud with trumpets and cymbals and the musical instruments of God. Now the sons of Jeduthun were gatekeepers. (1Ch 16:42) NKJV*

Worship is not dependent upon instruments, but they are certainly a very important part of it. The Lord has gifted and blessed individuals with musical gifts that are to be used in His house for His worship. This is a truth that is so wonderfully revealed by the Lord in the Tabernacle of David.

TRUE WORSHIP INVOLVES THE LIFTING OF HANDS.

> *I desire therefore that the men pray everywhere, lifting up holy hands, without wrath and doubting; (1Ti 2:8) NKJV*

> *Let my prayer be set before You as incense, The lifting up of my hands as the evening sacrifice. (Psa 141:2) NKJV*

The lifting of hands is another physical declarative act. It again lets the Spirit dictate to the flesh what the body will do in worship. In the Old Testament the priests would lift their hands as part of the wave offering.

In the New Testament the lifting of hands forms part of our sacrificial worship unto the Lord. It involves taking a position of both surrender and dependence.

TRUE WORSHIP INVOLVES SINGING.

> *A Psalm of Thanksgiving. Make a joyful shout to the LORD, all you lands! Serve the LORD with gladness; Come before His presence with singing. (Psa 100:1-2) NKJV*

> *Then David spoke to the leaders of the Levites to appoint their brethren to be the singers accompanied by instruments of music, stringed instruments, harps, and cymbals, by raising the voice with resounding joy. (1Ch 15:16) NKJV*

Our voices are for far more than talking. God has created us with an ability to sing, and we are to use it to worship Him. It is not dependant on our vocal ability, but on our willingness to give unto the Lord the honour He deserves.

TRUE WORSHIP INVOLVES BOWING.

> *All the angels stood around the throne and the elders and the four living creatures, and fell on their faces before the throne and worshiped God, (Rev 7:11) NKJV*

In bowing, we fall on our faces before the Lord in worship. In bowing we make ourselves lower as we lift Him higher and exalt His greatness. Bowing is another physical declarative act where we fall in honour before the true King.

TRUE WORSHIP INVOLVES CLAPPING.

> *To the Chief Musician. A Psalm of the Sons of Korah. Oh, clap your hands, all you peoples! Shout to God with the voice of triumph! (Psa 47:1) NKJV*

Though we may not all be talented musicians, God has blessed us with the ability to still make a noise in worship. With clapping our hands become the instruments of our worship.

TRUE WORSHIP INVOLVES DANCING.

Praise Him with the timbrel and dance; ...(Psa 150:4) NKJV

Then David danced before the LORD with all his might; and David was wearing a linen ephod. (2Sa 6:14) NKJV

We may not all be gifted with a natural rhythm but worship was never meant to be a stagnant or static action. In true worship there is a freeness where we have a spiritual freedom to worship the Lord in movement. King David is a great example of this.

The above points all form the boundaries surrounding the truth of worship that the Word reveals to us. All of these things are what the Word tells us worship should look like. These are elements of true worship, and these should all be part of the worship that we offer unto the Lord. Whilst these are all elements of truth, their representation in each service will not necessarily be equal and nor will their representation be exactly the same each week. There will be times where the Spirit leads a focus on bowing. There will be times where the Spirit leads us to dance. There will be times of loud and triumphant clapping and there will be times when clapping is quieter and sparse. Each of these are truth, but their volume and focus will vary as the Spirit leads. There is no pattern but there is an outline of truth within which the Spirit leads and operates. When we worship in Spirit though, within the bounds of truth, these elements should all be evident.

The nature of man would look at the above aspects of true worship and then make a checklist to ensure that all of these occur in our worship service. These become a benchmark for us to be able to know that we have performed true worship. We have done that, check. We have done that, check. True worship, check. But that is not true worship. To do that would be to do worship in truth but not necessarily in Spirit! The fact of the matter is that there is no magic formula, no checklist that we can check off.

What scripture gives us is the bounds that truth provides and then the Spirit leads us within these. True worship is worship that is in Spirit and in truth.

Whilst scripture does not give us the repetitive structure that we look for to know we are doing things right, scripture does however reveal to us that there is a clear sign from the Lord when our worship has met the standard of true!

Solomon's Example

In the books of Kings and Chronicles we read of the completion and subsequent dedication of the Temple of Solomon. This was the first time that a permanent dwelling had been erected for the worship of the Lord. It was something that king David had longed to do, but the task itself was entrusted to Solomon. 2 Chronicles 5-8 details this occasion for us and within it there are a number of things for us to pick up on as we look at the worship that was involved in this great event.

THE ARK WAS MOVED.

Up until this time the Ark of the Lord had remained in the Tabernacle of David. It had not again been moved. What we see though is that Solomon had learned from his father's mistakes. There was no presumption in how Solomon handled the Ark, all was done according to the truth of the word.

> *So all the elders of Israel came, and **the Levites took up the ark**. Then they brought up the ark, the tabernacle of meeting, and all the holy furnishings that were in the tabernacle. **The priests and the Levites brought them up**. Also King Solomon, and all the congregation of Israel who were assembled with him before the ark, were **sacrificing** sheep and oxen that could not be counted or numbered for multitude. Then the priests brought in the ark of the covenant of the LORD to its place, into the inner sanctuary of the temple, to the Most Holy Place, under the wings of the cherubim. (2Ch 5:4-7) NKJV*

Just like with David's second attempt, the Ark was carried upon the shoulders of the priests and sacrifice was carried out as the Ark was transported. That which represented the presence of the Lord was treated with the reverence that it deserved. All was done according to the truth of the Word. As the Ark was moved the priests made continually sacrifices unto the Lord, but such was the magnitude of what was offered the number of sacrifices could not be counted. There was a Spirit led generosity in the worship that was offered. The sacrifices were offered according to the truth of the Word, but the magnitude of them was through a leading of the Spirit. Spirit and truth were in harmony.

THE WORSHIP.

Once the Ark of the Lord was placed in the Most Holy Place, we read of the worship that took place. This was the worship that David had instituted with the Tabernacle of David:

> *and the Levites who were the singers, all those of Asaph and Heman and Jeduthun, with their sons and their brethren, stood at the east end of the altar, clothed in white linen, having cymbals, stringed instruments and harps, and with them one hundred and twenty priests sounding with trumpets— indeed it came to pass, when the trumpeters and singers* **were as one, to make one sound to be heard in praising and thanking the LORD**, *and when they lifted up their voice with the trumpets and cymbals and instruments of music, and praised the LORD, saying: "For He is good, For His mercy endures forever," that the house, the house of the LORD, was filled with a cloud, (2Ch 5:12-13) NKJV*

The musicians and singers were as one, to make one sound in praising and thanking the Lord. There was a unified voice in the worship that occurred. There was no evidence of the flesh, but rather a Spirit led unity. All were as one as they praised and thanked the Lord. There was one purpose, one sound and one focus.

The result of this we are told is that the House of the Lord, The Tabernacle of Solomon, was filled with the glory of the Lord.

> *that the house, the house of the LORD,* **was filled with a cloud**, *so that the priests could not continue ministering because of the cloud; for the glory of the LORD filled the house of God.*
> *(2Ch 5:13b-14)*

The glory of the Lord filled the house! How amazing this must have been for all in attendance. But it doesn't stop there!

SOLOMONS PRAYER.

The next detail for us to pick up on is with the prayer that Solomon prayed unto the Lord in 2 Chron 6:12-13:

> *Then Solomon stood before the altar of the LORD in the presence of all the assembly of Israel, and spread out his hands (for Solomon had made a bronze platform five cubits long, five cubits wide, and three cubits high, and had set it in the midst of the court; and he stood on it, knelt down on his knees before all the assembly of Israel, and spread out his hands toward heaven);*
> *(2Ch 6:12-13) NKJV*

The picture here is of Solomon in the court of the Temple, standing before the altar of the Lord on a bronze platform that he had commissioned to be made. Solomon then knelt down upon this platform, spread forth his hands towards heaven and began to pray. As we read this passage, we see a king who is declaring to the people he reigns over who the true King is. In supplication and humility, he comes before the Lord, publicly acknowledging His Lordship. It is a public testimony of the faith of Solomon.

If we take a moment to dive a little deeper, we actually see a greater truth revealed in this act of Solomon. The Bible never reveals details by accident. With that in mind we may ask ourselves, why is the platform that Solomon prayed on recorded and described in such detail? It wasn't part of the Temple furniture and is not again mentioned. So why would it be important to record that this platform was made of bronze and measured 5 cubits long by 5 cubits wide by 3 cubits high?

*(for Solomon had made a **bronze** platform **five cubits long, five cubits wide, and three cubits high**, and had set it in the midst of the court; ......(2Ch 6:13)*

If we jump back to the book of Exodus, we read of another piece of furniture that shared these exact same measurements and material:

*"You shall make **an altar** of acacia wood, **five cubits long and five cubits wide—the altar shall be square— and its height shall be three cubits**. You shall make its horns on its four corners; its horns shall be of one piece with it. And you shall overlay it with **bronze**. (Exo 27:1-2) NKJV*

The Brazen Altar in the Tabernacle of Moses measured the exact same measurements as Solomons platform and was constructed of the exact same material!

	BRAZEN ALTAR	**SOLOMONS PLATFORM**
LENGTH	*5 Cubits*	*5 Cubits*
WIDTH	*5 Cubits*	*5 Cubits*
HEIGHT	*3 Cubits*	*3 Cubits*
MATERIAL	*Overlaid with Bronze*	*Bronze*

The Brazen Altar was the altar where all sacrifice occurred. The Brazen Altar of Moses Tabernacle was not used in the Temple of Solomon, a new, larger altar was constructed for the Temple according to the designs that the Lord gave to David. And it was before this larger altar that Solomons platform stood. Everything in Solomons Temple was planned for and constructed with purpose. There are no coincidences in the Bible and what we see here was not an instance of chance. Solomons platform was a replica of the Brazen Altar in the Tabernacle of Moses! What we see here is Solomon offering himself as a living sacrifice as he kneels, hands spread out to heaven, upon the brazen platform. This was a significant act, and one that encapsulates the truths of Romans 12:1 that we discussed earlier. Solomon as king and representative of the nation of Israel, is presenting himself in worship as a living sacrifice unto the Lord upon a brazen altar.

Within this worship at the dedication of the Temple of Solomon we see true worship:

- We see worship that was done in Spirit and in truth.
- We see a reverence for His presence as the Ark was handled according to the Word of the Lord.
- We see a spirit led generosity in the sacrifices that were giving according to the truths of the Word.
- We see a Spirit led unity in worship as the priests all played with one accord, making one sound.
- We see the glory of the Lord fill the house as He came and inhabited the praises of His people.
- We see complete and total sacrifice of self, as Solomon offered himself unto the Lord.

It is an incredible picture that we are presented with, but what is more incredible is what happens next.

> *When Solomon had finished praying,* **fire came down from heaven and consumed the burnt offering and the sacrifices; and the glory of the LORD filled the temple.** *And the priests could not enter the house of the LORD, because the glory of the LORD had filled the LORD's house. When all the children of Israel saw how the fire came down, and the glory of the LORD on the temple, they bowed their faces to the ground on the pavement, and worshiped and praised the LORD, saying: "For He is good, For His mercy endures forever." (2Ch 7:1-3) NKJV*

This occurred after Solomon had finished praying. To recap, the Ark was brought up and sacrifices were made, the priests had worshipped in unity and the Lord had responded, Solomon had offered himself as a living sacrifice and then, after all of this, the fire of the Lord came down and consumed the sacrifices that were offered, and the glory of the Lord filled the temple. It is a consecutive series of events that led to this outcome.

The above passage details two incredible things that happened in response to the true worship that was offered. The fire of the Lord fell, and the glory filled!

THE FIRE OF THE LORD.

In scripture we see that the fire of the Lord falls in either acceptance of sacrifice or in judgement against sin. In the above passage we see that the fire of the Lord falls as a sign of acceptable sacrifice. This is a truth that we see numerous times throughout scripture:

- In 1 Kings 18 when Elijah confronted the prophets of Baal upon Mount Carmel, the fire of the Lord fell upon Elijahs sacrifice, as a sign unto the nation of Israel of who was God. No fire fell on the sacrifice of the prophets of Baal. Fire only fell on the sacrifice that was acceptable. (1 Ki 18:38)

- In Levitus 9 we are told that at the completion of the consecration of Aaron and his sons to the ministry that the fire of the Lord came out and consumed the burnt offering that was upon that altar. (Lev 9:24)

- When Gideon presented his offering before the angel of the Lord, fire consumed that which had been presented. (Judg 6:22).

- Whilst not explicitly stated, it is likely that the fire of the Lord fell and consumed Abel's offering showing that Lords acceptance and favour of it compared to that of Cains.

When the fire of the Lord comes upon that which was been sacrificed unto Him in worship it is a sign of His acceptance of true worship. The fire of the Lord is His seal upon that which has been offered. "Yes, this is true worship".

THE GLORY OF THE LORD.

On two occasions at the inauguration of the Temple of Solomon we are told that the glory of the Lord filled the building. It filled the building after the Ark of the Lord was brought in and it filled it again after Solomons prayer. The same glory that had been in the Tabernacle of Moses was now in the Temple of Solomon.

The glory of the Lord is the presence of God. It is God dwelling amongst His people. His glory enshrouds Him and when He comes to His people, it is the glory of the Lord coming amongst His people. God's presence comes when His people are united together in their worship of Him. It is the unity of His people in worship that creates the space for His glory to come and inhabit the praises of His people. This same truth is given to us by Jesus:

> *For where two or three are gathered together in My name, I am there in the midst of them." (Mat 18:20) NKJV*

The Lord showed up, because the worship of Solomon and the people of Israel was true worship done in spirit and in truth. It was the true worship that the Father was looking for.

So, from this example of Solomon, we see that both the glory of the Lord and the fire of the Lord come when His people are offering true worship in spirit and in truth. When our worship reaches the standard of true, God cannot but show up. It is His sign, His seal and His testament that what has been offered is true worship. His glory comes and His fire falls when our worship meets His standard of true.

The Church Born

We see this same truth again evidenced on the great day of Pentecost. In Acts 2 we read:

> *When the Day of Pentecost had fully come, they were all with one accord in one place. And suddenly there came a sound from heaven, as of* **a rushing mighty wind, and it filled the whole house** *where they were sitting. Then there appeared to them divided* **tongues, as of fire, and one sat upon each of them**. *And they were all filled with the Holy Spirit and began to speak with other tongues, as the Spirit gave them utterance. (Act 2:1-4) NKJV*

Several things should stand out to us from this:

THE UNITY OF THE PEOPLE.

They were gathered together with one accord in one place. There was unity. Just as there was with the priestly musicians and singers in the example of Solomon, so it was here. The disciples were gathered in the upper room according to the command of Jesus for them to wait in Jerusalem until they had received the promised baptism of the Holy Spirit (Acts 2:4-8). While they waited, we are told that they continued in prayer and supplication (Acts 2:14). This was not just a casual gathering. This was a gathering of individuals who were united in their worship and seeking of the Lord.

THE GLORY OF THE LORD.

A mighty rushing wind was heard, and it filled the house. How did they know it filled the house? The winds presence within the house must have been tangible. There was a change to the atmosphere of the room. This wind was the wind of the Spirit, and it filled the house with the glory of the Lord. His glory turned up.

THE FIRE OF THE LORD.

After this, there appeared tongues of fire that rested upon each individual. Why tongues of fire? And why did they rest upon each individual? Because the fire of the Lord is the sign of an acceptable sacrifice. Like Solomon, each individual had presented themselves as a living sacrifice unto the Lord, and here the fire of the Lord came upon each individual in acceptance of what they had presented. These individuals had dedicated their lives to the service of the Lord and the fire of the Lord came and rested upon them in acceptance of this.

Again, we see the truth, that **THE GLORY** of the Lord **AND HIS FIRE** fall upon true worship.

When our worship is true worship, it will be marked by both the fire and the glory of the Lord. Whilst there is not a check list for how to perform true worship, there is a sure-fire sign that our worship meets the Father's standard for true worship (pun slightly intended). The glory of the Lord will always inhabit true worship, and the fire of the Lord will always rest on that which is acceptable. True worship will be marked by both the glory of the Lord and the fire of the Lord!

It is interesting to note that in the example of Solomon's Temple and the great day of Pentecost, that the glory of the Lord always preceded the fire. The glory showed up, but there was a lag between the fire coming. For me this would be a prompt that sometimes we as New Testament Christians can get satisfied when the glory of the Lord has turned up. We have worshipped and He has entered our midst. Worship feels good. But there is a call to push beyond this. We need to wait for His fire. It is both His glory and His fire that reveal that our worship has been in spirit and in truth.

The questions that would flow from this are that if we are not experiencing His presence and His fire are we fulfilling the call of true worship? Is our worship meeting the standard of true? If it is not, what do we need to change?

The truth of the matter is that there is a discernible difference between the satisfaction of the flesh in worship and the acceptance of the Lord. Our flesh can feel good without the glory and the fire of the Lord! Our flesh is satisfied with a much lower bar. Our flesh is satisfied when its needs are met, and it feels good. But that is not true worship and nor is it the sign of true worship. True worship is in spirit and in truth and is ever marked by the glory and the fire of the Lord. If that is not our experience, then we need to examine our worship!

It is only when our worship is in spirit and truth that we will be able to meet the standard of true worship. As we operate within the boundaries of the Word with the freedom and leading of the Spirit that we offer unto the Lord the kind of worship He is looking for. Our worship has to have both! We are to be a people who worship in spirit and in truth. When we do this, **HIS GLORY AND HIS FIRE** will be evident in our lives and Churches.

The Lord is Seeking

But the hour is coming, and now is, when the true worshipers will worship the Father in spirit and truth; for the Father is seeking such to worship Him. (Joh 4:23) NKJV

Possibly the sentence that should resonate in the heart of every believer the most from our look at John 4 is contained in this verse. The Father is seeking true worship from those that worship Him! As the Lord looks upon His believers, He looks for those that are worshipping in truth.

To seek means to actively look for someone or something. It is not a passive action. The individual who is seeking is invested in what they are looking for and they keep looking until they find it (Luk 15:8). That is what the Lord is doing. He is actively looking unto His people for true worship that is in spirit and in truth. He is looking for His people to meet the standard of true. Such should implore each and every one of us to be those who meet the Lord's standard. Such should place such a burden in each of our hearts to be a people who not only worship the Lord but worship Him in spirit and in truth. It should birth a passion within us to worship the Lord with every fibre of our being. The Lord is seeking, how can we not respond?

It is not that the Lord has simply laid out a requirement of man to meet. He does not sit back and judge man on whether or not he has achieved true worship. The Lord is seeking true worship because true worship invites Him in. He stands at the door and knocks seeking to join us. When we offer true worship, we open that door and allow Him into our lives and services. As we saw in our previous section true worship will see His glory come in and His fire pour out. The Lord actively looks for those who offer true worship so that He may respond.

As believers there is a standard of worship that the Lord is seeking from us. It is a heavenly standard. Worship is actually something that originated in heaven. Long before man was created, there was worship in heaven. True worship. Throughout the Word of the Lord, God has revealed the standard of this worship to us. From Genesis through to Revelation the Lord has shown to man how He is to worship. The truths are all there and the Lord looks out for those who have received and applied this truth. He is looking for those that have understood this heavenly standard and offer unto Him true worship. The Lord is seeking out those who would worship Him in spirit and in truth.

Final Thoughts

In this study we have looked at the account of John 4 and that which we have deemed the standard of true. We have seen that as believers we are called to be those who worship in spirit and in truth. It is a call for each and every one of us.

In response to what has been presented some we may ask but doesn't God look on the heart? That is true, God does look at the heart. That is actually a statement that comes from Samuel's encounter with the Lord when he anointed David as the future king:

> *But the LORD said to Samuel, "Do not look at his appearance or at his physical stature, because I have refused him. For the LORD does not see as man sees; for man looks at the outward appearance,* **but the LORD looks at the heart***." (1 Sa 16:7) NKJV*

From this verse it could be argued that if God looks on the heart, then when He looks at our worship, He is looking to see what our heart attitude is in it. It is not so much what we offer, whether it is in spirit and in truth, but it more how we offer it, i.e. our heart attitude.

Now it is true that the Lord looks at the heart, but the context of this verse is on the character of man rather than his charisma, i.e. the outward appearance he portrays. This verse looks at how man looks at man and how God looks at man in terms of the calling of God. That is what was happening in 1 Samuel 16. Samuel was looking at the sons of Jesse to see whom the next king of Israel would be. As Samuel did this, he looked toward the appealing attributes of David's brothers, and it was for this that the Lord rebuked him. The Lord told Samuel that He didn't look at the outward appearance in regard to the stature of David's brothers, but He looked at the heart and for this reason had selected David as the next king of Israel. The Lord doesn't look at what man thinks would qualify an individual; He looks at the heart!

This particular verse does not apply to worship. To do so is to take this verse out of context. If this verse did apply to worship, then there would have been no issues when David followed the example of the Philistines in bringing the Ark of the Lord up the first time on a cart. David was a worshipper and had the heart of a worshipper. David's heart was right so therefore His worship must have been true. From our look at this account though we know that this was not the case. If God was looking solely at the heart of David in worship at that moment, then we would not have had the same outcome! David was a man after God's own heart (Acts 13:22) and yet despite this fact, we see that from this example that Davids worship in error was not blessed! The Lord wasn't looking at David's heart, He was looking to see if His people were worshipping Him in spirit and in truth! David's intentions and worship were honourable. His heart was to do a good thing and his motivation was pure, but the Lord could not bless his actions for they were in error. God cannot bless that which is contrary to His truth.

It is very clear from scripture that in terms of worship the Lord has clearly laid out how He is to be worshipped. The Lord has told us that He is looking for true worshippers and whilst our hearts may be right, if we are not worshipping in spirit and in truth then we are not meeting the standard of true. The Lord has shown us how we are to worship, and He is looking for His people to approach Him in this way.

The purpose of this study has not been to condemnatory or judgemental in any way, but it has sort to express the burden that the Lord has placed upon my heart. The Lord is wanting to stir His people. Our heavenly Father is looking for true worship and He is calling His people to be those who would worship Him in spirit and in truth.

FINAL THOUGHTS

It is my prayer that I have been able to communicate this clearly and that you in turn have been both stirred and challenged in your spirit to be one who worships in spirit and in truth. Ours is not to set the standard but it is ours to meet it. May we ever be a people who offer unto the Lord the true worship that He deserves.

May we be a people who offer true worship, worshipping in spirit and worshipping in truth.

Blessings in Christ,

Courtney

Worship In Flesh + Worship In Error ≠ True Worship

Worship In Spirit + Worship In Error ≠ True Worship

Worship In Flesh + Worship In Truth ≠ True Worship

ONLY

Worship In Spirit + Worship In Truth = True Worship

AND

Will be attested to and confirmed by the <u>Glory</u> and the <u>Fire</u> of the Lord

Bibliography

- The Authorised King James version of the Bible, Public Domain.
- Scriptures takes from the New King James Version. Copyright ©1982 by Thomas Nelson, Inc. Used by permission. All rights reserved
- Strong, James. The New Strong's Expanded Exhaustive Concordance of the Bible. Thomas Nelson, 2010
- Laird, C.A. Way Error Rebellion, *A Call for Course Correction.*

Other Books by the Author

If my people, which are called by my name, shall humble themselves, and pray, and seek my face, and turn from their wicked ways; then will I hear from heaven, and will forgive their sin, and will heal their land. (2Ch 7:14)

In 2 Chronicles we read of the temple of the Lord being built by King Solomon after many years of planning and preparation by King David. Just after the Temple's dedication, we read in 2 Chronicles 7:11-16 that the Lord spoke to Solomon through a dream. It is the words of the Lord to Solomon in this dream that form the basis of this study. As we examine this dialogue, we discover that there are a number of biblical truths that flow from this encounter.

If My People examines what these truths are and follows them through scripture before considering their application to the Church. The call of the Lord in 2 Chronicles is one that echoes to the Church of today. The precedent that the Lord set forth to Solomon has application to us as believers. Within the pages of this study we well discover how the call of "If My People" applies to the Church of today and the responsibilities that come with it. The Lord has much for His Church and His people if they can fulfill His call of "If My People".

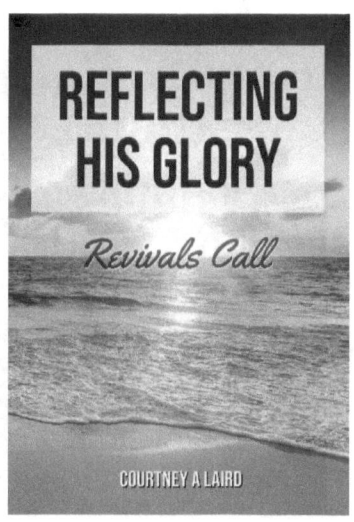

Were we made to reflect His Glory? How do we shine in a world that seems so dark? What is Revivals Call?

This text considers the call that exists within scripture for believers individually and corporately as the Church, to shine and reflect the glory of the Lord in the areas where He has planted them. As we investigate this call, we see that there is not only an onus on believers and churches to shine, but there is also a process laid out in scripture for how this occurs. The Lord not only calls us to shine, He shows us how to fulfill this call! Through examining this process, we learn not only how we reflect His glory and shine, but also what is seen when we do and ultimately what happens to the world around us when we reflect the glory of the Lord brightly.

It is my belief that we are in a time when the Lord is stirring His people and His Church to shine as brightly as they have been called to. There is a call of the Lord unto His people in this day. It is Revivals Call. The Lord is calling His people to a new depth of relationship, one where we will reflect His glory as brightly as we have been called to. If we will respond to this call of revival, then we will see the Lord move in mighty ways and

In the epistle of Jude we read that within the Church there was a negative influence, seeking to corrupt and undermine the beliefs and foundations of the believers there. In addressing the individuals who were responsible for this Jude states:

> *Woe unto them! for they have gone in the way of Cain, and run greedily in the error of Balaam for profit, and perished in the rebellion of Korah. (Jud 1:11)*

In describing the individuals at fault, Jude specifically refers to three Old Testament events and the individuals who were responsible for them. What did Jude mean by this and what implication did if have to the Church at the time? Does it have any application to believers and the Church today? These are questions that we will seek to answer as we look in the Word of God and examine Jude's statement.

www.ingramcontent.com/pod-product-compliance
Lightning Source LLC
Chambersburg PA
CBHW031243290426
44109CB00012B/416